pure® food

pure® food

EAT CLEAN WITH SEASONAL, PLANT-BASED RECIPES

Veronica Bosgraaf

founder of Pure Bar

CLARKSON POTTER/PUBLISHERS
NEW YORK

Published in the United States by Clarkson Potter/Publishers, an imprint of the Crown Publishing Group, a division of Random House LLC, a Penguin Random House Company, New York.
www.crownpublishing.com
www.clarksonpotter.com

Library of Congress Cataloging-in-Publication Data
Bosgraaf, Veronica.
Pure food / Veronica Bosgraaf. — First edition.
pages cm
Includes index.
1. Cooking (Natural foods). 2. Seasonal cooking. 3. Sustainable living. 4. Kitchens. I. Title.
TX741.B627 2015
641.3'02—dc23 2014004886

ISBN 978-0-8041-3795-9
eBook ISBN 978-0-8041-3796-6

Printed in the U.S.A.

Book design by La Tricia Watford
Jacket design by La Tricia Watford
Jacket photography by Quentin Bacon

10 9 8 7 6 5 4 3 2 1

First Edition

Contents

Introduction

Most people would assume that one of the reasons I wrote a cookbook is because I am a trained chef. How I more accurately define myself—which probably many of you can relate to—is as a very busy mother of three kids who works many hours and is under a lot of pressure (self-created, no doubt) to feed her family well and at least try to live a semi eco-conscious life. When someone calls me a great cook, I sometimes feel like an imposter because most of what I cook is extremely simple. But the beauty of it is I have found that creating healthy and fabulous food does not have to be complicated, and that is what I want to share with you.

It takes time to learn confidence in the kitchen, and I got there in an unusual way: by starting a business. In 2006 I started Pure—a line of all-natural, organic snack bars made with fruits, nuts, and spices—out of my home, and without formal culinary or business training. The business came about as a direct result of my daughter, who when she was six years old announced that she was a vegetarian. Yes, one night at dinner, out of the blue, she made this proclamation, and instead of shrugging her off, I decided to validate her decision and learn more about a vegetarian lifestyle. I began to rework the things I cooked, looking for ways to rely more on fruits and vegetables while packing in lots of important vitamins and nutrients. One day, I started playing with a pie crust recipe (the original recipe is on page 116), adding extra ingredients, and ended up with a delicious, all-natural snack that became very popular with my family and friends. This became the first Pure Bar. Convinced I was onto something, I went out on a limb and sought out a manufacturing company that would mass-produce my product, eventually finding a mom-and-pop plant in the far corner of Oregon that was willing to give me a chance. I began with 4,500 Pure Bars, and over the next several years, grew my business to where my Pure Bar was nationally distributed at fantastic stores like Whole

Foods and Trader Joe's. It's been such a blessing to see it succeed!

Starting my business the way I did—with no real training for it—taught me that anything is within my reach. And that includes cooking! Growing up watching two remarkable women—my mom and my grandmother—cook everything from scratch is how I have learned. And through experimenting and a little creativity, I am able to create delicious foods packed with the nutrients my family and I need to stay strong and healthy all year long.

Pure Food is not a "fancy" cookbook. It's an approachable guide to help you quit fast, frozen, processed foods and get back into the kitchen. This book isn't full of snack-bar recipes, but instead demonstrates how I feed myself and my family on a daily basis. My recipes are simple and wholesome, and use real, seasonal foods that hopefully will help others rediscover cooking, and do it within their schedule. Granted, there are some more challenging recipes in the book because we all need to be pushed out of our comfort zone, but even those are recipes for real people who don't think they have the time or confidence to cook.

In this book I have assembled recipes that make the most of ingredients when they're at their peak, which is why they're organized by month of the year. I live and grew up in Michigan—a Midwestern, agricultural state that has plenty of meat and dairy. And yet I follow a vegetarian diet. Eating this way makes my body feel good, and aligns with my beliefs too. Although I'm not a stickler for vegan or gluten-free eating, I have included several recipes that abide by these tenets.

I believe that life is about balance and it is more important to eat clean, real food than to be overly strict about never eating this or that (unless, of course, you have an allergy). Here, I have taken many of my favorite recipes from my childhood and given them a "makeover," switching out processed ingredients for fresh, seasonal ones. I tested everything on my kids and friends, all Midwestern salt-of-the-earth people. I am not some fanatic, but rather the girl next door—or, I guess, the mom next door now—who is trying to do the right thing for her family.

I think we have a lot more cooking ability in us than we give ourselves credit for. Yes, you can make an amazing Peach Raspberry Crostata from scratch (page 156), organic Homemade Almond Milk (page 34), a vegan Strawberry Ice Cream Pie (page 116), or glorious Avocado Pesto (page 89). These are the foods I eat often. When others ask me how I stay fit and energized, I tell them it is almost entirely because of the amazing foods I choose to eat. But it's not a hard choice; it is something anyone can easily do.

I believe in you and your ability to become an accomplished cook and to make healthy, nutritious meals anytime. I know you can do it and will feel so great about it, too!

The Pure Pantry

The most important rule I have for cooking is to use real ingredients: fresh items not found in a can or jar or box. Real food is free of synthetic additives and has been spared manufacturing processes that break down or extract beneficial nutrients. There is less packaging waste as well. It is simply better for our bodies and better for the environment to buy this way.

I also try to buy local, seasonal, and organic. Buying local, seasonal food means my food is fresher and my money supports local farmers. Local and seasonal go hand in hand and provide a unique combination of fruits and vegetables, which have essential nutrients that our bodies need. Buying organic is also extremely important to me. As the founder of a company that creates organic products, I am well versed in the vast advantages of buying a certified organic product over a product that is not. The organic ingredients are not sprayed with harmful chemicals to control weeds and bugs. In addition to contaminating our bodies, chemical sprays pollute our soil, streams, rivers, lakes, and oceans and negatively affect the health of farmworkers who are constantly exposed to them.

Organic ingredients are also not allowed to be grown with genetically modified seeds. I am very against eating genetically modified organisms (GMOs), and many crops like corn and soy have been manipulated in this manner (see page 203 for more information). Buying organic is a good safeguard against these substances, though I recommend also looking for the non-GMO seal.

alternative ingredients

Besides cooking with whole foods as much as possible, I try to find healthier alternatives to common ingredients. I truly had no idea how many great healthy substitute ingredients are out there until I started experimenting. For example, different flours allow you to rework recipes to be gluten free, and coconut oil can be substituted for butter and other oils in some recipes, making them healthier. I purposely use a variety of flours, sweeteners, and oils in my recipes so that you can see how they behave and decide for yourself which ones you prefer to work with. Here is some information on the alternative ingredients I like to use and why.

alternative sweeteners

Typical white sugar is bleached with an array of chemicals and stripped of its minerals. White sugar is also often filtered with bone char, from the bones of cows, and therefore is unsuitable for vegans and many vegetarians.

I use HONEY whenever I can because to me it is the most natural sweetener. Unrefined honey provides minerals, has antibacterial properties, and has been shown to help reduce the symptoms of gastroesophageal reflux disease (GERD) and intestinal distress.

MAPLE SYRUP is slightly processed, but it is still natural and more robust in flavor than honey. It also contains more minerals and fewer calories. It has high concentrations of zinc and manganese, which provide immune support.

Similar to maple syrup, AGAVE NECTAR is minimally processed and contains natural substances that boost our immune system and have anti-inflammatory properties.

ORGANIC CANE SUGAR offers the most similar taste to that of processed white sugar, yet it is much less processed and made from sugarcane that is grown without pesticides. It is also never processed with bone char. I often grind this sugar in my food processor to make it very fine so that I can use it in place of fine baking sugar and even confectioners' sugar.

ORGANIC CONFECTIONERS' SUGAR is simply finely ground organic cane sugar with a bit of tapioca starch added to prevent clumping. I avoid conventional confectioners' sugar because it goes through the same chemical-laden growing and refining process as white sugar does.

ORGANIC BROWN SUGAR is organic cane sugar with molasses. You can actually make your own brown sugar by adding 1 tablespoon of molasses to 1 cup of organic cane sugar and mixing well.

alternative flours

WHITE WHOLE-WHEAT FLOUR is made from a blend of spring and winter wheats. White whole wheat has a lighter taste and texture than standard whole wheat. It is a good substitute for all-purpose flour.

MILLET FLOUR has a light and mild flavor and is excellent for baking.

BUCKWHEAT FLOUR is actually not related to wheat and contains no gluten. It has a strong grassy flavor and, when baked, produces a dense product. It is best when used together with one of the lighter flours.

COCONUT FLOUR, made from coconut that has been defatted and dried, has a slight coconut flavor that works well with many baked goods. Coconut flour is almost always mixed with other flours because it doesn't have sufficient structure for proper baking.

BROWN RICE FLOUR has a slightly nutty taste, is darker in color than white rice flour, and when combined with white rice flour makes a good substitute for wheat flours.

WHITE RICE FLOUR is a finer and more delicate version of brown rice flour in texture and taste. It can be used alone or in combination with heavier flours for a lighter final product.

QUINOA FLOUR has a strong, earthy taste but is very nutritious. I try to sneak it in with other flours if I can, but I tend to use it cautiously because of its strong flavor.

alternative oils

COCONUT OIL has amazing brain-boosting fats that actually reduce your appetite, help you burn more energy, increase the good cholesterol in your system, and help you fight infections. I buy unrefined, organic coconut oil, and I often use it instead of butter or any other oil.

GRAPESEED OIL, OLIVE OIL, AND OTHER PLANT-BASED OILS are great, too. I use a variety of organic unrefined oils depending on my cooking needs. See page 24 for more information on oils.

alternative milks

ALMOND MILK is hands down my favorite! I make a homemade version (page 34) that is a hundred times more delicious than cow's milk. Almond milk is natural milk that our bodies can easily digest. It has more than nine naturally occurring vitamins and minerals, as well as antioxidants that may help prevent aging and certain cancers. All of the following milk alternatives are free of casein, an animal protein found in cow's milk, which is linked to respiratory problems and an increase in cancer. In my recipes calling for almond milk, I use either my homemade recipe or the store-bought "original" variety of Silk almond milk, unless I specify otherwise.

SOY MILK is something I don't use much because I feel the flavor is strong and overtakes recipes. When I do use it, I always buy organic and non-GMO because more than 90 percent of the soy grown in the United States is genetically modified. Soy milk is rich in protein and also provides essential vitamins and minerals.

RICE MILK is a great alternative for people who have nut or soy allergies but want dairy-free milk. It is lower in fat and calories but higher in carbohydrates than cow's milk. It provides some vitamins and minerals as well as important antioxidants from its grain.

Of all the milk alternatives, HEMP MILK is the nutritional superstar. It provides a wide variety of vitamins and minerals, as well as antioxidants and omega-3 fatty acids, which are important for brain and cardiovascular health. Hemp milk has a distinct flavor and does not work in all recipes, but it is worth making and trying yourself. Try my Strawberry Hemp Milk Shake on page 70.

COCONUT MILK is filled with an array of vitamins and minerals and is an excellent substitute for dairy in your recipes. You can buy it to drink like almond milk or in a can for cooking. I always buy the full-fat version because I enjoy the taste more and it's better in recipes. Try it in my Coconut Boysenberry Smoothie on page 153.

january

Coconut Cranberry Porridge

Lemon Ricotta Pancakes

Fresh Ginger Juice

Roasted Root Vegetables with Honey Sauce

Winter Garlic and Vegetable Stew

Warm Potatoes and Spinach with Rosemary Dressing

Lentils and Rice with Caramelized Onions

Cacao Chip Banana Bread

Chocolate Rice Pudding

Buckwheat Crepes with Butterscotch Bananas

I've noticed that having kids forces you to become a kid again in many ways. For example, you find ***yourself playing outside*** in a massive blizzard when only a few years ago you would've been locked in your house with the shades drawn, hibernating under a blanket and cursing the weather. My experience has been that my children make me act younger, and in a good way.

Seeing life through the ***eyes of my children*** gives me a totally different perspective, and it certainly helps me get through the long Michigan winters. I always tell my friends in California that it's actually an advantage to have the kind of weather that forces you to be indoors because while they are all out surfing, we have nothing to do but think and create.

This is why ***winter is one of my favorite times*** to be in the kitchen. Standing at the stovetop working on a pot of warm, hearty soup, like my Winter Garlic and Vegetable Stew (page 21), is the perfect place to be when it's dark and cold outside. Cooped up inside for the month of January, I can ***experiment with recipes*** and come up with healthier versions of old favorites, as I did with my Cacao Chip Banana Bread (page 26). Take advantage of time at home and rediscover ***your own creativity***.

JANUARY

Here is a sample menu I've put together with a variety of recipes for this month.

breakfast

Lemon Ricotta Pancakes

•

lunch

Lentils and Rice with Caramelized Onions

•

midday snack

Cacao Chip Banana Bread

•

dinner

Winter Garlic and Vegetable Stew

•

dessert

Chocolate Rice Pudding

Coconut Cranberry Porridge

In my January kitchen, I strive to experience the diverse and colorful flavors of the season yet not infringe on any newly made or consistent health resolutions. The first morning back to work or school after the holidays, I love to make this porridge. The smell of toasting coconut and the meditative stirring that goes into making it set my year off right. It is a good hearty breakfast that is delicious on its own, though I sometimes sprinkle on spices like cinnamon, cloves, turmeric, or nutmeg, too.

serves 4

½ cup fresh cranberries

1 tablespoon coconut oil

2 tablespoons coconut flakes (sweetened or unsweetened), plus more for serving

1 cup steel-cut or whole oats

½ teaspoon sea salt

2 tablespoons maple syrup, or to taste

Coconut or almond milk, for serving

1. In a blender, combine the cranberries and 2 cups of water and blend for 20 seconds.
2. In a medium saucepan set over low heat, melt the coconut oil. Add the coconut flakes and cook, stirring, until the coconut begins to brown, 1 to 2 minutes. Add the cranberry mixture, oats, and salt. Raise the heat to medium-high and bring the mixture to a boil. Reduce the heat to medium-low and cook, stirring occasionally, until thick and creamy, about 25 minutes.
3. Remove the pan from the heat and slowly stir in the maple syrup. Serve with the coconut milk drizzled over the top and a sprinkling of coconut flakes.

Lemon Ricotta Pancakes

Have you ever eaten such an amazing dish at a restaurant that you find yourself wishing you could mimic it in your own kitchen? If so, then do it! One thing I have learned from being an entrepreneur is that formal training is not a must for success. I have never taken a business class and yet have been able to launch and run my business. If you have a passion for something, then you are already an expert on so many levels.

This recipe was inspired by a delicious breakfast at one of my favorite seaside restaurants in California. I have to admit that after a few tries I think this version came out even better than the original. I especially love the pomegranate seeds sprinkled on top!

serves 4

8 ounces ricotta cheese

4 large eggs, separated

Grated zest of 1 lemon

1/8 teaspoon grated nutmeg

1/8 teaspoon sea salt

2 tablespoons organic cane sugar

4 1/2 tablespoons grapeseed oil

Organic confectioners' sugar, for garnish

1/3 cup pomegranate seeds, for garnish

Juice of 1 lemon (optional)

1. In a medium bowl, whisk together the ricotta, egg yolks, lemon zest, nutmeg, and salt.
2. In the bowl of an electric mixer fitted with the whisk attachment, beat the egg whites at medium speed until foamy, about 2 minutes. Add the sugar and beat to incorporate. Increase the mixer speed to high and beat until stiff peaks form, about 5 minutes. Gently fold the egg whites into the batter.
3. Heat 1 1/2 tablespoons of the oil in a large, heavy nonstick skillet set over low heat. When the oil begins to sizzle, add the batter, 1/4 cup per pancake, and cook until golden brown on the bottom, about 2 minutes. Flip the pancakes and cook until the second side is browned, about 1 more minute. Transfer the pancakes to a plate and cover loosely with foil to keep them warm. Repeat with the remaining oil and batter.
4. To serve, sprinkle the pancakes with the confectioners' sugar and pomegranate seeds, and sprinkle the lemon juice over the top, if desired

Fresh Ginger Juice

When my youngest was two years old, he would walk around with a sippy cup filled with this green-colored juice. People would stare and sometimes ask, "What in the world is in there?" They could not believe their ears when I told them kale, pear, ginger, and cranberries!

Anyone with a juicer will attest to the fact that there is no taste comparison between freshly juiced fruits and vegetables and store-bought juices. This is a great way to get vegetables like kale into everyone's diet! Kale is *the* superstar green, with off-the-chart levels of vitamins K, A, and C, as well as calcium, iron, and protein.

serves 2

1 bunch kale

3 large Anjou pears, cored and cut into 8 wedges

½ cup fresh cranberries

⅛-inch piece fresh ginger

1 cup fresh orange juice (optional)

Feed the kale through a juicer, followed by the pear, cranberries, and ginger, and serve. Alternatively, purée the kale, pears, cranberries, and ginger in a blender with the orange juice. Strain the juice through a sieve (or for less pulp, through a piece of cheesecloth) and serve.

tip *why you should invest in a juicer*

Juicers can be expensive, but I encourage you to try to save up or even buy one as a "family Christmas present" because it will benefit the health of your family in massive ways for years to come. There are many brands on the market, and I use one made by Greenstar.

By separating the pulp and skin from the juice of fruits and vegetables, juicers allow you to drink a very concentrated form of these nutrient-rich foods. Fresh juice delivers unbelievable flavor and unadulterated nutrients in a very absorbable form that your body can then utilize to keep you healthy. Store-bought juice has been heated, stored, reheated, and often mixed with additional sugars and flavors. Juicers help you get right to the good stuff!

Roasted Root Vegetables *with* Honey Sauce

One Saturday morning, I woke up and realized that I had forgotten that we had a family gathering at my mom's house and I was responsible for bringing vegetables. I had only two hours before we had to leave! I opened the refrigerator and saw some carrots, a few turnips, and a couple of yellow beets. Because I always have onions, I decided to gather them along with the rest of the motley crew, chop them all up, and roast them until nice and caramelized. While the veggies were in the oven, I created a simple sauce to serve with them. The recipe ended up being a big hit. Who knew?

serves 6

2 medium turnips, peeled and chopped

2 medium yellow beets, peeled and chopped

4 medium carrots, chopped

2 medium onions, chopped

1 tablespoon grapeseed oil

1 teaspoon sea salt

2 tablespoons (¼ stick) unsalted butter or vegan buttery spread

2 tablespoons honey

Juice of 1 small lemon

½ teaspoon turmeric

½ teaspoon ground cinnamon

1. Preheat the oven to 375°F.
2. In a large bowl, toss together the turnips, beets, carrots, onions, oil, and salt. Spread the vegetables out in a 9 × 13-inch glass baking dish.
3. Roast, stirring occasionally, until the vegetables are tender, about 45 minutes. Remove the dish from the oven.
4. In a small saucepan set over low heat, combine the butter and honey, stirring until melted. Remove the pan from the heat and stir in the lemon juice, turmeric, and cinnamon. Pour the sauce over the vegetables and toss to coat. Cover the baking dish with foil. Put the dish into the still-warm oven for 15 minutes.
5. Serve hot.

Winter Garlic *and* Vegetable Stew

On Sunday afternoons, I love to put on some music, chop vegetables, and get a big yummy pot of comfort stew going. There is nothing like the warm scent of simmering onions and garlic to create a cozy atmosphere. It's funny to me that my kids claim to not like onions, and yet whenever I simmer onions in a little grapeseed oil, one by one they start to drift into the kitchen and say, "Mom, it smells so good in here." It never ceases to amaze me how flavorful and hearty winter vegetables are, and the carrots, potatoes, cauliflower, and cabbage in this stew make it a filling meal. I like to serve this with Stewed Apples (page 189) and whole-grain bread.

serves 6

3 tablespoons grapeseed oil

1 large onion, chopped

8 garlic cloves, cut in half lengthwise

½ teaspoon turmeric

½ teaspoon ground cumin

3 large carrots, sliced into ½-inch-thick rounds

5 medium red potatoes, chopped

1 head orange cauliflower, coarsely chopped

½ head purple cabbage, coarsely chopped

2 medium tomatoes, cored and chopped

1 cup vegetable broth, homemade (see Tip, page 183) or store-bought

1 teaspoon sea salt, plus more to taste

Freshly ground black pepper

1. Heat the oil in a large pot set over low heat. Add the onion, garlic, turmeric, and cumin, and cook, stirring, until the onions are soft, about 10 minutes. Add the carrots, potatoes, cauliflower, cabbage, tomatoes, broth, and 1 teaspoon salt. Bring to a simmer and cook until the vegetables are tender, about 45 minutes.

2. Season to taste with salt and pepper and serve.

Warm Potatoes *and* Spinach *with* Rosemary Dressing

Potatoes and rosemary are a match made in heaven! I like a dish that doesn't play by the rules, too: Is this a salad or a side dish, or even a main dish? It can be all of them. My favorite way to serve this is with warm bread, olive oil, and freshly shaved Parmesan for lunch.

serves 4

DRESSING

¼ cup extra-virgin olive oil

1 tablespoon fresh lemon juice

1 tablespoon agave nectar

½ teaspoon finely chopped fresh rosemary

Sea salt and freshly ground black pepper

SALAD

4 large red potatoes, thinly sliced

1 teaspoon sea salt

2 cups lightly packed baby spinach leaves

½ medium red onion, thinly sliced

¼ cup pine nuts

1. For the dressing, combine the olive oil, lemon juice, agave, and rosemary in a bottle or jar with a secure lid. Shake well. Season with salt and pepper to taste.

2. Put the potato slices in a large skillet and add enough water to cover the potatoes. Add the salt, set the pan over medium-low heat, and bring to a simmer. Cook until the potatoes are tender but not mushy, about 5 minutes. Drain the potatoes and keep them warm.

3. Arrange the spinach leaves on a platter. Top with the warm potato slices, red onion, and pine nuts. Drizzle the dressing evenly over the top. Season with salt and pepper and serve immediately.

tip homemade laundry detergent

The one thing I hate to buy at the grocery store is laundry detergent because I think it is way too expensive for what you get. That's why when my brother and his wife told me they make their own detergent for pennies, I listened. The recipe uses Fels-Naptha soap, which is petroleum based. Personally, I think that Fels-Naptha soap is very harsh and I prefer to use a plant-based soap (coconut oil). It may slightly reduce the effectiveness on stains, but I keep a stain remover product on hand and also pretreat stains with some of the homemade laundry soap and some elbow grease.

Remember, too, that we generally use too much soap in our laundry. I've heard eco experts talk about how most Americans measure their laundry soap above the line provided by the company, when in truth even the suggested amount tends to be too much. Soap residue is a magnet for dirt and dust, so if you are using too much soap you are doing yourself a disservice.

makes almost 2 gallons

1 (4-ounce) bar Kirk's Original Coco Castile soap, grated

½ cup borax

½ cup Arm & Hammer washing soda

1. In a large pot set over medium-high heat, combine the grated soap and 6 cups of water. Heat, stirring, until the soap is dissolved, about 5 minutes. Add the borax and washing soda and stir until dissolved.

2. Pour the mixture into a bucket filled with 1½ gallons of warm water. Stir well and let sit for 24 hours. As the soap sits, it becomes more gel-like. Use ½ cup per regular load of laundry.

tip *choosing the right oil*

Not all cooking oils are created equal. With so many oils on the market, it can be really difficult to know which to use, so I rely on simple guidelines. If I am going to sauté, roast, or pan-fry using medium to high heat, I choose grapeseed oil. It has a mild flavor, can be purchased organic and non-GMO, and has a high smoke point (425°F). Sesame oil and sunflower oil are also good for high-heat cooking.

The "smoke point" is the threshold of heat where oil breaks down and starts to smoke. The smoke releases dangerous chemicals into the air and the food. So make sure you cook with an oil that has a high smoke point.

I don't use olive oil to sauté, pan-fry, or roast because it has a lower smoke point and the smoke point is less consistent depending on how the oil is processed. I use olive, walnut, or pumpkin oil as a flavorful finishing oil for salads or for cooking at very low temperatures.

Lentils *and* Rice *with* Caramelized Onions

Some of the most amazing lessons I've learned in the kitchen have come from my wonderful neighbor Fadi, who is Lebanese. Fadi has taught me much about the foods he grew up with in Lebanon—things like lentils, olive oil, lemons, cherries, yogurt, olives, and hummus—as well as how they combine into delicious dishes that satisfy the body's need for nutrients. Fadi comes straight from a culture of simple, healthy meals made from basic, local ingredients. I try to emulate this idea in the recipes I create for my family.

serves 4

¼ cup olive oil

2 medium onions, chopped

1 cup brown lentils

1 teaspoon sea salt

1 cup basmati rice

Sea salt and freshly ground black pepper

1. Heat the olive oil in a large saucepan set over low heat. Add the onions and cook, stirring, until the onions are very soft and sweet, about 15 minutes. Stir in the lentils, ½ teaspoon of the sea salt, and 4 cups of water. Bring to a boil, reduce the heat to medium-low, and simmer until the lentils are tender, about 40 minutes.
2. Stir in the rice, the remaining ½ teaspoon salt, and 2 cups water. Cover the pan and simmer until all of the water is absorbed and the rice is tender, about 20 minutes.
3. Season with salt and pepper to taste and serve.

Cacao Chip Banana Bread

When I was little, I had a babysitter who would make banana bread with chocolate chips in it. I thought it was positively sinful and the best idea I had ever heard of! Then I grew up and thought that I simply couldn't eat such a treat every morning if I wanted to be healthy and stay fit. Or could I? The beauty of learning to cook is that you begin to understand that the flavors and textures of bad-for-you foods can be replaced with similar flavors and textures from good-for-you foods. For this recipe, I replaced white flour with a healthier white whole-wheat variety, and regular chocolate with raw cacao chips, which are the most unadulterated and unprocessed form of chocolate.

makes three 3 × 5½-inch loaves

½ cup grapeseed oil, plus more for pans

2 cups white whole-wheat flour

1 teaspoon baking soda

½ teaspoon ground cinnamon

½ teaspoon sea salt

3 medium ripe bananas

2 large eggs

⅔ cup agave nectar

1 teaspoon vanilla extract

½ cup cacao chips

1 cup coarsely chopped walnuts

1. Preheat the oven to 300°F. Grease three 3 × 5½-inch loaf pans with oil.
2. Sift the flour, baking soda, cinnamon, and salt into a medium bowl, and set aside.
3. In the bowl of an electric mixer fitted with the paddle attachment, beat the bananas, eggs, agave, oil, and vanilla. Gradually add the flour mixture and beat until incorporated. Add the cacao chips and ¾ cup of the walnuts, and beat until just combined. Divide the batter among the prepared pans. Sprinkle the tops with the remaining ¼ cup walnuts.
4. Bake until the loaves are puffed and a wooden skewer inserted into the center comes out clean, about 40 minutes. Remove from the oven and let cool for at least 10 minutes. Serve hot, warm, or at room temperature.

Chocolate Rice Pudding

I am from the generation that grew up on Jell-O instant pudding. From tapioca to chocolate, vanilla to freakishly green pistachio, instant pudding was the dessert of choice in our family, and it is still a comfort food to me. But I had to find a way to make it without all the sugar and dairy. Rice pudding is naturally thick and creamy, and it's good for your body because it's a simple grain. When combined with healthy, rich ingredients like coconut oil, maple syrup, vanilla, and cocoa, you end up with a decadent yet wholesome dessert.

serves 4

½ cup short-grain white rice

⅛ teaspoon sea salt

1 tablespoon coconut oil

2 cups almond milk, homemade (page 34) or store-bought, plus more if needed

¼ cup maple syrup

½ teaspoon vanilla extract

1 tablespoon raw cacao powder or cocoa powder

1 cup raspberries or pomegranate seeds, for serving

1. In a medium saucepan set over low heat, combine the rice, salt, oil, and almond milk. Cook, stirring, until the mixture begins to boil, about 7 minutes. Cover the pan and cook until the rice is soft, about 15 minutes. Add more milk for a more liquid consistency.
2. Meanwhile, whisk together the maple syrup, vanilla, and cacao powder. Add it to the rice and stir well. Remove the pan from the heat and let the pudding cool for 10 minutes. Cover and chill for 2 hours.
3. To serve, top with the raspberries.

Buckwheat Crepes *with* Butterscotch Bananas

How about dessert that doubles as a breakfast? I love these crepes because they are more gourmet than pancakes. Sometimes I serve them with crushed berries and whipped coconut cream or maple syrup. I can make them in my kitchen as quickly as any pancake or waffle batter, and my family enjoys them as well.

serves 4

CREPES

1½ cups almond milk, homemade (page 34) or store-bought

2 large eggs

1 large egg white

2 teaspoons maple syrup

1 tablespoon grapeseed oil, plus more for skillet

½ cup millet flour

⅓ cup buckwheat flour

1 tablespoon tapioca starch

Pinch of sea salt

SAUCE

½ cup fresh orange juice

¼ cup maple syrup

1 tablespoon dark rum

¼ cup organic cane sugar

3 bananas, cut diagonally into ¾-inch-thick slices

1. For the crepes, in a large bowl, whisk together the almond milk, eggs, egg white, maple syrup, and oil.

2. In a small bowl, combine the millet flour, buckwheat flour, tapioca starch, and salt. Add the dry ingredients to the almond milk mixture, ¼ cup at a time, beating between additions, until incorporated.

3. Set a medium nonstick skillet or griddle over medium heat. Brush with a little oil and pour a scant ⅓ cup of batter into the skillet, swirling the skillet to coat the bottom. Cook until the edges are golden and the batter on top looks cooked, about 2 minutes. Turn the crepe out onto a piece of waxed paper, browned-side up. Keep warm. Repeat with the remaining batter, whisking the batter if it separates.

4. For the sauce, in a small skillet set over high heat, combine the orange juice, maple syrup, rum, and sugar. Bring to a boil, reduce the heat to low, and simmer, stirring, until slightly thickened, about 4 minutes. Add the bananas and cook, occasionally turning the bananas, until they begin to brown, 1 to 2 minutes.

5. To serve, fold the crepes in half and in half again, and put them on dessert plates. Spoon the bananas and sauce over the crepes and serve immediately.

tip *the art of breathing*

Did you know that you can lower your stress by the simple act of breathing? Taking slow, deep breaths sends a message to the body to relax and calm down. It also oxygenates your cells and brain, which can help you focus. This is one of the reasons why meditation is so good for you, but even taking a few deep breaths throughout the day can help you live in an overall more relaxed state. So take a long, deep breath and blow a kiss good-bye to anxiety!

february

Homemade Almond Milk

Easy Vegan French Toast

Jicama with Roasted Red Pepper Hummus and Dulse

Kale Slaw with Apples

Dill Havarti Couscous with Rainbow Chard

Vegan Tacos

Toasted Almond, Leek, and Sprout Stir-Fry

Raw Chocolate Chip Cookies

Chocolate Soufflé with Grandma's Chocolate Sauce

I was ***born on Groundhog Day,*** which is something my brothers never let me forget. These days, I embrace that fact. I channel my inner groundhog and try to predict the coming of spring. I think I even occasionally do a better job than Phil (as in Punxsutawney Phil, the famous weather-predicting groundhog). I'm kind of glad my birthday falls in February, because it gives me ***something to look forward to*** in the middle of Michigan winters.

February is when I first start to hear the birds again. The days get noticeably longer, and even though it is very snowy where I live, the month has a delightful feeling about it. It is about lighting fires and snuggling with your loved ones. It is about gathering in warm pubs with your friends while the wind and snow lash around outside. There is a comfort in this month of love, and the meals we prepare can enhance this warmth. So even if my inner groundhog says we have more than six weeks of winter left, there is still so much to enjoy!

FEBRUARY

Here is a sample menu I've put together with a variety of recipes for this month.

breakfast

Easy Vegan French Toast

•

lunch

Dill Havarti Couscous with Rainbow Chard

•

midday snack

Raw Chocolate Chip Cookies

•

dinner

Vegan Tacos

•

dessert

Chocolate Soufflé with Grandma's Chocolate Sauce

Homemade Almond Milk

In Venice, California, there was a man who called himself the "Mylkman." He delivered homemade almond milk to your door. I *loved* his almond milk and noticed that he only used fresh coconut water and almonds, two amazingly healthy ingredients. Unfortunately, I live in Michigan, where I can't get a Mylkman delivery, but there aren't exactly palm trees dropping coconuts in my yard. So to make my own almond milk, I had to use store-bought coconut water, which is very expensive. I set out to mimic coconut water in nutrition and flavor for a *much* cheaper price. I think I hit the nail on the head because everyone in my house fights over this milk. I often make two batches, one sweetened with maple syrup and one without, so that I can use the unsweetened version for vegan cream sauces and other savory dishes.

makes about 6 cups

2 cups raw almonds

4 cups filtered water, plus more for covering almonds

2 tablespoons coconut oil

2 tablespoons maple syrup

½ teaspoon vanilla extract

⅛ teaspoon sea salt

1. Put the almonds in a large bowl, cover with filtered water, and let soak for 4 to 8 hours.
2. Drain the almonds and put them in a blender. Add the 4 cups of fresh filtered water, the coconut oil, maple syrup, vanilla, and salt. Purée until smooth.
3. Strain the milk through a piece of cheesecloth into a glass jar or pitcher. The almond milk will keep in an airtight container in the refrigerator for up to a week.

tip *homemade almond flour*

What to do with the wonderful almond pulp that you have left over from your very easy and delicious almond milk? Do not throw it away or even compost it. There are several recipes in this book alone that call for almond meal and almond flour, which are essentially the same thing. In my opinion, almond meal is a bit chunkier and almond flour is ground smooth, but I use them interchangeably and always grind mine smooth when I make it.

Set your oven to its lowest setting. After making almond milk and squeezing out the pulp, spread the pulp on a rimmed baking sheet. Put the pan in the oven and heat it, stirring occasionally, until it is dry and crumbly, about 3 hours. Remove the pan from the oven and let cool. Transfer the pulp to a food processor and pulse to the desired consistency. The almond flour will keep in an airtight container in your refrigerator for up to a week.

makes about 2 cups

Easy Vegan French Toast

French toast has been a staple in our house for a long time. I always made it the traditional way with eggs, milk, butter, and cinnamon, and I couldn't figure out for the longest time how to make a vegan version. But my almond milk (page 34) is the perfect fix. The coconut oil in the milk helps the bread brown nicely, and the almond particles give the dish great substance. I usually use the last bit of milk in the container because it gets thicker as it sits. It's a super-easy dish, but the only thing I am careful with is soaking the bread. Because bread absorbs almond milk more readily than eggs and milk, I instead brush the almond milk on so that the bread doesn't get soggy.

serves 4

½ cup Homemade Almond Milk (page 34), strained or unstrained

4 slices sourdough bread

Ground cinnamon, for sprinkling

Maple syrup, warmed, for serving

1. Pour the almond milk into a shallow bowl.
2. Heat a large nonstick griddle over medium heat. Put the bread slices on the griddle and brush each side with the almond milk until fully coated but not soggy. Sprinkle the upward-facing side with the cinnamon. Cook until the first side has browned, 4 to 5 minutes. Flip the bread slices and sprinkle the other side with cinnamon. Cook until the second side has browned, 1 to 2 minutes.
3. Serve with warm maple syrup.

tip coconut oil spray

If you want the convenience of a cooking spray for greasing your pots and pans, try an organic coconut oil spray. Conventional cooking sprays contain unhealthy chemical additives and GMOs from the soy that is added to them. They can also contain artificial flavors. Organic coconut oil spray remains stable at high temperatures and organic versions are much cleaner and safer to ingest. I like to use Kelapo Organic brand because it is also a soy-free and fair-trade product.

Jicama *with* Roasted Red Pepper Hummus *and* Dulse

This is a terrific recipe to have in your back pocket because it is one of those appetizers that makes you look like a gourmet chef, yet is so easy you can whip it up in minutes. Besides that, it proves that you don't need meat, butter, cream, or even sugar or salt to make a wildly flavorful and hearty snack. I love introducing people to the sweet and crunchy taste of jicama, which I often use in stir-fries, in Veggie "Sushi" Roll (page 108), and in place of crackers. I also adore the deep salty flavor of dulse seaweed (but don't tell diners it's seaweed until after they've eaten it), which can be found at natural food stores.

To make plain hummus, omit the roasted red peppers. You may need to add a tablespoon or two of cold water while processing to achieve a nice smooth texture.

serves 6

HUMMUS

1 (15-ounce) can chickpeas

1 tablespoon tahini

1 teaspoon chopped garlic

3 tablespoons olive oil

1/8 teaspoon sea salt

1 tablespoon fresh lemon juice

1/2 cup jarred roasted red peppers

1/2 teaspoon sumac

1 jicama, peeled and sliced into 2-inch pieces

1 cup dulse seaweed leaves, torn into 1-inch pieces

Cayenne pepper, to taste

1. For the hummus, in a food processor, combine the chickpeas, tahini, garlic, olive oil, salt, lemon juice, red peppers, and sumac. Blend until smooth.
2. Spoon a dollop of hummus onto each jicama slice. Top with a dulse leaf and sprinkle with cayenne pepper. Serve immediately.

tip *add it at the end!*

I always try to add spices and oils—and even juices—at the end of cooking. Heat will start to break them down and they may lose nutritional value as well as taste. Whether it's drizzling with pumpkin oil, sprinkling with cinnamon, or spritzing with fresh lemon juice, I spare these precious ingredients the heat to make sure they are as flavorful and nutritious as can be.

Kale Slaw *with* Apples

Kale, citrus, sesame seeds, and apples are some of my favorite winter ingredients. Kale and citrus are two of the most powerful foods for our bodies. I always feel like these two ingredients were designed to be winter foods because they protect our bodies so well during the months when colds and sicknesses are prevalent. In fact, it's remarkable to me how many foods are perfectly suited for the season they are available in. There is an order and a purpose behind nature's bounty, and it's another reason why eating seasonally just makes sense.

When eating raw kale, I often squeeze lemon juice over it and rub it in until the kale is softer.

serves 4 to 5

2 tablespoons sesame seeds

Grated zest of 1 orange

¼ cup fresh orange juice

1 tablespoon fresh lemon juice

2 tablespoons sesame oil

Sea salt and freshly ground black pepper

1 bunch kale, coarsely shredded

1 large carrot, grated

1 Gala or Fuji apple, cored and very thinly sliced

1. In a small skillet set over medium heat, toast the sesame seeds, stirring often, until lightly golden, 2 to 3 minutes. Transfer to a plate and set aside.

2. In a large bowl, whisk together the orange zest, orange juice, lemon juice, and sesame oil, and season with salt and pepper to taste. Add the kale, carrot, apple, and sesame seeds, and toss well. Serve immediately or chill.

Dill Havarti Couscous *with* Rainbow Chard

My grandma Otten loved dill Havarti cheese. After immigrating to the United States as a young girl, she settled with her family in the dairy country of Wisconsin. There, she grew up and worked as a governess, creating and learning all sorts of wonderful tricks in the kitchen that she passed on to my mother and me.

One thing Grandma always used to say was, "Don't take the whole bottle of aspirin." So as I attempt to eat less dairy, I don't cut out my absolute favorites. Life is too short for serious deprivation! Grandma always served dill Havarti with sliced radishes, olives, and pickles, and this cheese always reminds me of her. I love the indulgence and comfort of this recipe, yet know I am still eating great foods that give my body the nutrients it needs, including high amounts of antioxidants from the rainbow chard. Life is about balance!

serves 4

½ cup pine nuts

1 cup filtered water

¼ teaspoon sea salt, plus more to taste

1 cup couscous

2 tablespoons grapeseed oil

1 bunch rainbow chard, tough stem ends removed and sliced (about 4 cups loosely packed

Freshly ground black pepper

1½ tablespoons fresh lemon juice

1 tablespoon chopped fresh dill

1 cup shredded dill Havarti, for garnish

1. In a medium saucepan set over medium heat, toast the pine nuts until golden, 2 to 3 minutes. Transfer to a plate and set aside.
2. In a small saucepan set over high heat, combine the water and salt and bring to a boil. Remove the pan from the heat, stir in the couscous, and cover. Let stand for 5 minutes.
3. Meanwhile, heat 1 tablespoon of the oil in a large skillet set over medium heat. Add the chard and cook, stirring constantly, until barely wilted, about 2 minutes. Add the couscous and toss well. Season with sea salt and pepper. Mix the remaining 1 tablespoon grapeseed oil with the lemon juice and dill, and drizzle over the couscous. Toss in the pine nuts.
4. Serve hot, at room temperature, or chilled, garnished with the Havarti.

Vegan Tacos

If you fix tacos from a kit bought at the store, you must stop. Tacos are so easy to make from scratch, and I will make it even easier for you. You probably have all the makings for taco seasoning in your kitchen cupboard right now. Once you have a great spice blend, you have many choices for how you want to make tacos. If you are feeling the need to mimic ground beef tacos, you can spice up organic, non-GMO soy meat, as I do in this recipe. If you want to stay with just veggies, slice and sauté some peppers for a fajita-like meal. If you want to use legumes, you can add this seasoning to lentils, refried beans, or black beans. So many options!

serves 6

TACO SEASONING

2 tablespoons chili powder

1 teaspoon Simply Organic All-Purpose Seasoning

1 teaspoon paprika

1 teaspoon ground cumin

1 teaspoon sea salt

⅛ teaspoon cayenne pepper

1 tablespoon cocoa powder (optional)

GUACAMOLE

2 avocados, peeled, pitted, and chopped

1 medium tomato, cored and chopped

1 small onion, chopped

½ cup loosely packed fresh cilantro leaves

Juice of 1 lime

Sea salt

TACO FILLING

1 tablespoon grapeseed oil

1 onion, chopped

1 tomato, cored and chopped

1 (10-ounce) package non-GMO soy crumbles

Taco seasoning (above)

½ cup coffee or water

Soft or hard taco shells, for serving

1. For the taco seasoning, in a small bowl, combine the chili powder, all-purpose seasoning, paprika, cumin, salt, cayenne, and cocoa powder, if using. Set aside.

2. For the guacamole, in a medium bowl, combine the avocado, tomato, onion, cilantro, lime juice, and salt. Mash to your desired consistency. Cover and refrigerate until ready to serve.

3. For the tacos, heat the grapeseed oil in a skillet set over medium-low heat. Add the onion and cook, stirring, until soft, about 10 minutes. Add the tomato, soy crumbles, and taco seasoning and stir to combine. Add the coffee a little at a time, stirring well until the mixture is moist. Simmer until the flavors meld, about 10 minutes.

4. To build the tacos, put the veggie and soy crumble mixture in the taco shells and top with the guacamole. Serve immediately.

tip *processed veggie meat*

I hate the word *processed*. I'm sure you do, too. Any food that has been torn apart and put back together is just not as good for you as the whole food. That being said, as a vegetarian it is nice to be able to cook with a ground beef or chicken substitute occasionally, if it meets a few requirements.

The most important requirements are that it's certified organic and made with ingredients that are not genetically modified. I know from owning an organic food business how strict the requirements are for ingredients, cleanliness, and machinery. There are also many rules that prevent the addition of artificial and synthetic ingredients. Also, I feel very strongly against the use of GMO, or genetically modified, ingredients. See page 203 for more information on non-GMO products.

Veggie meat substitutes can also be helpful for your kids. It is hard to deny kids some of the foods that are so popular for children. I would never serve a chicken nugget to my kids, but I do occasionally buy chicken nuggets made with vegetable protein. They just want to feel like kids sometimes, and I don't want them to feel completely deprived.

Toasted Almond, Leek, *and* Sprout Stir-Fry

Last Christmas my mother-in-law gave me a jar full of mung beans. I had no idea what to do with them. Shortly after that, I picked up a bag of sprouts at the grocery store and made the connection (most bean sprouts are sprouted mung beans). This is how you know I am a regular person, not a chef!

I made this stir-fry recipe, which was awesome, but I wasn't impressed with the store-bought sprouts, so I decided to sprout my own. I know, I'm sounding like a foodie, but trust me when I say it was incredibly easy and definitely worth it. The beans take a couple of days, but thankfully you don't have to do much. Mung beans can be found online, at your local natural food store, or in Asian markets, often in the bulk section.

serves 4

2 cups long-grain rice

½ teaspoon sea salt

2 teaspoons sesame oil (cold-pressed, not toasted)

1 cup sliced almonds

1 cup sliced leek (white parts only)

2 cups mung bean sprouts (recipe follows)

1 teaspoon minced ginger

½ teaspoon balsamic vinegar

1 tablespoon maple syrup

Sliced pears, for serving

1. Combine the rice and 2½ cups of water in a rice cooker. Let the mixture stand for 2 hours. Add the salt and turn on your rice cooker. Cook for 15 to 20 minutes. Alternatively, if you don't have a rice cooker, prepare the rice on the stovetop according to package instructions.

2. Heat the sesame oil in a pan set over medium-low heat. Add the almonds and toast until just starting to brown, about 3 minutes. Reduce the heat to low and add the leeks, sprouts, and ginger. Cook, stirring, until the vegetables are warmed, about 30 seconds. Remove the pan from the heat. Add the balsamic vinegar and maple syrup and toss well.

3. To serve, divide the rice among 4 plates, spoon the stir-fry over the rice, and top with the sliced pears.

mung bean sprouts

1 cup dried mung beans

Put the mung beans in a mason jar and add 4 to 5 inches of water. Cover the jar and put it out of direct light. Mung beans will sprout best at a temperature above 70°F. Every day strain and rinse the beans and fill the jar with fresh water. The beans should sprout in 2 to 3 days. ***makes 2 cups***

Raw Chocolate Chip Cookies

This indulgent recipe was a winner in one of our Pure Vegetarian Recipe contests. It was created by Emily Davidson and has become a family favorite in our house! Like Pure Bars, these little nuggets are made with unheated ingredients and pressed together without cooking. Keeping the ingredients away from heat helps preserve their nutrients. I am always delighted at how simple and decadent this recipe is. My kids can easily make these cookies in the food processor and snack on them as treats. Try substituting different nuts and spices: add cocoa, cinnamon, lemon rind, or lavender. Play around with various combinations to create healthy sweets that treat your body right. For this recipe I like to use pitted dates that I pit myself because they stay softer that way. You can also soak them in filtered water for 10 minutes to soften.

makes 10 cookies

1 cup pitted dates
3/4 cup raw cashews
3/4 cup raw walnuts
1 1/2 tablespoons coconut oil
1/2 teaspoon sea salt
1 teaspoon vanilla extract
1/4 cup cacao nibs

1. Process the dates in a food processor until well chopped. Add the cashews, walnuts, coconut oil, salt, and vanilla and process until smooth. Add the cacao nibs and pulse to combine.
2. Using your hands, form the dough into 10 cookies. Chill in the fridge for about 1 hour to solidify before serving.

tip *coconut oil*

Coconut oil is a near perfect ingredient. I often use it in cooking because it adds healthy, delicious, plant-based fat to anything. I actually think it tastes like an Almond Joy candy bar. Try a spoonful and see for yourself! I also love to use straight cold-pressed coconut oil as a skin lotion and massage oil. The oil easily soaks into your skin and provides nontoxic, all-natural moisture. It also has antimicrobial effects to protect against infection and antioxidants that protect our skin from aging. It is February, the month of love, so get creative and think up all sorts of uses for this wonderful oil.

Chocolate Soufflé *with* Grandma's Chocolate Sauce

My grandma Otten used to make an amazing chocolate sauce that we would pour over everything of a dessert nature. Of course, it was so full of butter and processed sugar that it was definitely a no-no most of the year. Using minimally processed, whole, organic ingredients with no additives and no dairy, I was able to virtually duplicate it. It was a joyous day in my kitchen, and I actually like it better (sorry, Grandma!). I like to serve it over these delicious low sugar, gluten-free individual chocolate soufflés that only take about 15 minutes to make!

serves 4

6 tablespoons coconut cream

2 ounces organic dark chocolate (I like Green and Black 70% Dark Chocolate), chopped

¼ cup white rice flour

2 eggs

Grandma's Chocolate Sauce (recipe follows)

1. Preheat the oven to 400°F. Grease four 4-ounce ramekins and set aside.
2. Combine the coconut cream and dark chocolate in a double boiler and melt over low heat until smooth, about 5 minutes.
3. In a medium bowl, whisk together the flour and eggs until smooth. Add the chocolate mixture and stir well. Divide the batter evenly among the ramekins.
4. Bake until cooked through, about 10 minutes. Let cool for 10 minutes, drizzle 1 tablespoon of the chocolate sauce over each soufflé, and serve.

grandma's chocolate sauce

½ cup maple syrup

⅛ teaspoon vanilla extract

3 tablespoons raw cacao powder

⅛ to ¼ teaspoon sea salt

¼ cup coconut oil, melted

Using a fork, whisk together the maple syrup, vanilla, cacao powder, and salt. Add the melted coconut oil and whisk until blended and smooth. ***makes about ¾ cup***

march

Gluten-Free Coconut Pancakes

Pickled Vegetables

Bibb Lettuce with Grapefruit, Avocado, and Creamy Avocado Dressing

Scalloped Potatoes with Onion, Garlic, Peppers, Savory, and Dill

Creamy Vegan Cabbage Stew

Carrot and Curry Soup

Vegan Keema

Irish Hash

Vegan Orange Cream Pops

Warm Pear Crumble

Remember making calendars in grade school? We used cotton balls to make the mane of the March lion and the woolly coat of the end-of-the-month lamb. "In like a lion," March always seems it should be the mark of the end of winter, but where I live, it fools you into thinking the winter will last forever—at least in the beginning!

My daughter's birthday is in early March, and when I look back on pictures over the years, there is always still snow on the ground here in Michigan. Nonetheless, this month is when we get more ***sunny, snow-melting days*** with chirping birds. I always try to find a way to be outside on a sunny day, even if it's cold! I love the ***feeling of the sun*** on my face, my skin soaking up the bright, healing light.

This is also the time when I start thinking about gardening. What do I ***want to plant*** this year? Do I want to be ambitious or simple? For fun, I buy herbs to sit on my windowsill and miniature daffodils to remind me of what is just around the corner.

The ***flavors of March are eclectic***—a combination of the comfort food of winter and a hint of the beginning of spring. Foods like grapefruit, spinach, pears, peppers, cabbage, carrots, and orange cream pops fill my March menu. It feels good to anticipate the next chapter in the season!

MARCH

Here is a sample menu I've put together with a variety of recipes for this month.

breakfast

Gluten-Free Coconut Pancakes

•

lunch

Bibb Lettuce with Grapefruit, Avocado, and Creamy Avocado Dressing

•

midday snack

Vegan Orange Cream Pops

•

dinner

Vegan Keema

•

dessert

Warm Pear Crumble

Gluten-Free Coconut Pancakes

"Mom, what's for breakfast?" If I had a nickel for every time I heard that, I'd be retired. Good thing I have an answer with these light and healthy gluten-free coconut pancakes. I love working with coconut flour because it is rich and soft and smells delicious! Rice flour makes the pancakes delicate, and tapioca starch thickens the batter. I make them small so they are easier to flip, and cook them on low heat because they brown quickly.

Coconut flour, tapioca starch, and rice flour are sold at natural food stores, and it's easy to find organic brands. Although delicious on their own, these pancakes are great topped with sliced tropical fruits, such as pineapple, mango, and kiwi.

serves 4

2 cups almond milk, homemade (page 34) or store-bought

3 large eggs

¼ cup agave nectar

1 teaspoon vanilla extract

⅔ cup unsweetened shredded coconut

⅔ cup white rice flour

⅓ cup coconut flour

1½ tablespoons tapioca starch

1 teaspoon baking soda

¼ teaspoon kosher salt

Grapeseed oil, for griddle

1. In a medium bowl, whisk together the almond milk, eggs, agave, and vanilla.
2. In a separate large bowl, combine the shredded coconut, rice flour, coconut flour, tapioca starch, baking soda, and salt. Make a well in the center of the dry ingredients. Pour the almond milk mixture into the well and stir until just combined.
3. Heat a griddle over low heat. Lightly brush the griddle with grapeseed oil. Ladle 2 tablespoons of batter per pancake onto the griddle and cook until bubbles appear near the center, about 2½ minutes. Carefully flip the pancakes (they will be delicate) and cook until golden, about 1½ minutes. Repeat with the remaining batter.

tip *composting*

A very simple earth-friendly habit to cultivate at home is composting. I am always astounded by how much less garbage we have as a family. By composting, we recycle food rather than contribute to a landfill, and we create our own nutrient rich mixture to use in the garden and on the lawn in the process. When we first started composting at my house, my kids didn't like it. "Mom, that's gross!" They were paranoid that their friends would see our compost container and tease them about it, so we had to keep it out of sight. Over time, though, it became a normal part of what we do. I keep a simple plastic container with a lid in the kitchen, and about every other day one of us takes it outside to empty it into our compost bin that's behind the garage. Composting has cut our family trash amount in half!

Cooking with mostly fresh ingredients contributes to less overall waste as well. Fewer boxes equal more compost and less trash! Every week or so we "stir" the compost to mix it up. It quickly decomposes into a fibrous black matter. Then we add some of it to the soil in our garden every spring because it's a great fertilizer. This simple household habit offers a great lesson in how food can be recycled for the good of the land. Pass it on!

tip best indoor herbs

Herbs are nutrient powerhouses! Some of my favorites and the easiest herbs to grow inside are basil, rosemary, thyme, and oregano. With the days lengthening, March is a great time to start growing some herbs on a south-facing windowsill that you can plant in the garden later or just leave for decoration.

Start with seeds or seedlings from the grocery store. If your friends have oregano or rosemary, ask if you can take a cutting. Put it in water until the herb roots and then plant in soil. I use small clay pots with a drainage hole, and in the bottom of the pots, I layer small stones, clay, or broken dish pieces and top with good potting soil. Add the seeds and cover lightly with soil. Water the seeds well and keep the soil moist but not soggy. With good sunlight, they will sprout in no time!

Pickled Vegetables

I know you don't have hours to spend in the kitchen, but fear not! Pickling your own vegetables takes 10 minutes to prepare, saves money, and is a perfect solution when you need an extra side dish or appetizer for a party. Another bonus is that pickled vegetables are actually better for you than raw because the healthy bacteria that are created add more probiotics and vitamins.

My good friend Chef Ernest Miller, a Master Food Preserver from The Farmer's Kitchen in Los Angeles, turned me on to the ease and health benefits of pickled foods, which are essentially fermented. I learned this recipe from him. You can experiment with all sorts of vegetables, from peppers to green beans, and try changing up the spices, too!

serves 4 to 6

1½ pounds chopped cabbage, green beans, or vegetable of your choice

1½ teaspoons caraway seeds

1½ teaspoons mustard seeds

1 teaspoon celery seeds

3 tablespoons sea salt

1. In a large bowl, toss together the cabbage, caraway seeds, mustard seeds, celery seeds, and 1 tablespoon of the salt. Stuff the mixture into a mason jar with a lid.
2. In the same bowl, combine 4 cups of water and the remaining 2 tablespoons salt. Pour the brine over the cabbage. Use a smaller jar as a weight to keep the cabbage submerged. Loosely place the lid on the jar to allow the air to flow and put the jar in a warm place out of the sun (70°F to 80°F is optimal fermentation temperature; less than that will slow fermentation). Let sit for about 2 weeks.
3. After 2 weeks the pickled vegetables should be ready. If you prefer a more sour taste, let them sit longer.

Bibb Lettuce *with* Grapefruit, Avocado, *and* Creamy Avocado Dressing

I often eat a whole avocado in one sitting. I had a friend once tell me that I had better slow down or I would put on weight, but I never did slow down or put on weight. You see, my theory is that when you eat nutrient-dense, whole foods, you are giving your body what it needs and it will stay full and satisfied longer. You end up eating less. On the other hand, when we eat empty calories, we can't stop because our bodies are still craving nutrients. I think it is very difficult if not impossible to become overweight on a plant-based whole food diet, so keep eating those avocados!

serves 4

1 head Bibb lettuce

1 pink grapefruit, peeled and sectioned

1 medium avocado, peeled, pitted, and sliced

½ cup slivered almonds

Creamy Avocado Dressing (recipe follows)

1. Carefully remove the core of the lettuce, keeping the head intact. Rinse well, and then remove the leaves one at a time and lay them in a serving bowl.
2. Top the lettuce with the grapefruit, avocado, and almonds, and toss gently to combine. Top with the dressing and serve.

I love how nature gives us healthy fats that we can use to make creamy foods without the guilt. I could practically drink this dressing from the pitcher! Its beautiful bright green color will liven up any salad. I use grapeseed oil instead of olive oil because it is milder in flavor and lets the other ingredients shine through.

creamy avocado dressing

½ cup grapeseed or olive oil

1 tablespoon honey

1 garlic clove

1 medium avocado, peeled, pitted, and chopped

Juice of 1 lime

¼ cup fresh orange juice

Sea salt and freshly ground black pepper

In a blender, combine the oil, honey, garlic, avocado, and lime and orange juices, and season with salt and pepper. Purée until smooth. The dressing will keep in an airtight container in the refrigerator for up to 3 days. ***makes 1 cup***

Scalloped Potatoes *with* Onion, Garlic, Peppers, Savory, *and* Dill

Potatoes get a bad rap. I am always taken aback when I hear people who are trying to lose weight say, "I can't eat potatoes" or "I can't eat fruit," and then I watch as they microwave a prepackaged diet lunch. Eating whole foods is better than eating processed stuff any day because real food gives our bodies nutrients that haven't been overcooked, crushed, strained, dissolved, or changed in any way. I remember Grandma Otten's advice, "Eat food as close to its natural state as possible." That goes for potatoes, too! This simple recipe will make you glad you haven't given them up.

serves 4

2 tablespoons grapeseed oil

2 garlic cloves, chopped

1 medium yellow onion, chopped (about 1½ cups)

1 yellow or orange bell pepper, cored and thinly sliced

3 medium white russet potatoes, thinly sliced

½ teaspoon sea salt

½ teaspoon freshly ground black pepper

1 tablespoon chopped fresh savory, sage, or thyme

2 tablespoons fresh dill

1. Heat the oil in a large skillet set over medium-low heat. Add the garlic and onion and cook, stirring, until soft, about 10 minutes. Add the bell pepper, potatoes, salt, and pepper, raise the heat to medium, and cook, stirring, about 5 minutes. Add ½ cup of water, reduce the heat to low, and cook until the potatoes are tender, 20 to 25 minutes.

2. Remove the pan from the heat and stir in the savory and dill. Serve warm.

Creamy Vegan Cabbage Stew

Oh, is this ever a favorite from my childhood—a good Dutch tradition for sure! Cabbage is one of my favorite vegetables, and it's so versatile. It is also one of the most inexpensive vegetables. Here, I've reworked my mom and grandma's creamed cabbage recipe, vegan style! You can use the cream sauce base to make many other types of creamy sauces. Add vegetable broth to thin it out, if you wish. You can also add tomatoes, rosemary, or basil and use it to top veggies, potatoes, or pasta.

serves 6

½ teaspoon sea salt

1 large head cabbage, cored and coarsely chopped

CREAM SAUCE

2 tablespoons grapeseed oil

2 tablespoons all-purpose flour

½ cup unsweetened almond milk, homemade (page 34) or store-bought

¼ teaspoon grated nutmeg, plus more for serving

¼ teaspoon sea salt

Freshly ground black pepper

1. Bring 4 cups of water and the ½ teaspoon of salt to a boil in a large pot. Add the cabbage, return to a boil, reduce the heat to low, cover, and simmer until the cabbage is soft and bright green, 7 to 8 minutes.
2. Meanwhile, for the cream sauce, heat the grapeseed oil in a medium saucepan set over low heat. Add the flour and cook, stirring, until it forms a paste, about 2 minutes. Slowly add the almond milk and cook, stirring, until the paste fully dissolves, about 3 minutes. Add the nutmeg, salt, and pepper.
3. Drain the cabbage well and put it into a serving bowl. Pour the cream sauce over the cabbage and stir well. Sprinkle with a little more nutmeg and pepper, and serve.

Carrot *and* Curry Soup

Curry, carrots, and ginger create a soup that is creamy and delicious without an ounce of dairy! Using the right combination of ingredients is key to creating flavors that will satisfy your body without loading up on cream and butter. Plus, you get the amazing antioxidant value of the vegetables, spices, and herbs.

serves 4

8 medium carrots, cut into large pieces

½ cup chopped yellow onion

2 cups vegetable broth, homemade (see Tip, page 183) or store-bought

1 teaspoon curry powder

¼ teaspoon turmeric

¼ teaspoon ground ginger

2 tablespoons honey

2 cups unsweetened almond milk, homemade (page 34) or store-bought

1 tablespoon coconut oil

¼ teaspoon sea salt

1 avocado, peeled, pitted, and diced, for serving

1. In a saucepan set over medium-low heat, combine the carrots, onion, and broth. Bring to a boil and cook until the carrots are soft, about 15 minutes. Transfer the mixture to a blender. Add the curry, turmeric, and ginger. Blend until smooth, starting on a very low setting so as not to splatter the hot soup.

2. Return the soup to the pan. Add the honey, almond milk, coconut oil, and salt. Heat until warm, about 5 minutes. Divide the soup among bowls, garnish with the avocado, and serve.

tip curry

Curry is one of my favorite spices. It has been a part of my life from as early as I can remember. I owe this familiarity to my dad's parents, who were medical missionaries in Pakistan and India for forty years. Grandma and Grandpa boarded an ocean liner soon after graduating from nursing and medical school, respectively. Because they lived in that part of the world for so many years, my grandmother learned how to cook many amazing Indian dishes. And whenever we gather as an extended family we cook keema and dahl, poppers and vegetable curries. I often find myself cooking with curry at home and looking for the nearest Indian restaurants when I travel.

Curry is a blend of extremely nutritious spices, including turmeric, coriander, red pepper, and cumin. High in antioxidants and rich in calcium, potassium, and vitamin A, it has been shown in studies to help prevent Alzheimer's and certain cancers. It has also been shown to help prevent inflammation and joint degeneration due to arthritis. It's quite a health and flavor powerhouse!

Vegan Keema

The name of this recipe is an oxymoron because keema is a traditional Indian meat dish that's similar to a casserole, and *keema* actually means "minced meat." There are many ways to make keema, and I grew up eating it made with ground beef, tomatoes, and spices. Now I re-create the same flavors I crave using lentils instead of meat, and I like it even better. I make this dinner every other week or so. It is simply fabulous.

serves 6

2 tablespoons olive oil

1 medium onion, chopped

2 cups cooked lentils

2 medium tomatoes, cored and chopped

1 tablespoon curry powder, or to taste

½ cup coffee

½ plus ¼ teaspoon sea salt

2 cups baby spinach leaves or 1 cup frozen peas

2 cups basmati rice

¼ teaspoon saffron threads

1. Heat the oil in a medium skillet set over medium-low heat. Add the onion and cook, stirring, until soft, about 10 minutes. Add the lentils, tomatoes, curry, coffee, and ½ teaspoon of the salt. Cook until the mixture simmers, 5 to 10 more minutes, adding water if necessary to prevent sticking. Turn off the heat, add the spinach, stir, and cover. Let sit for 5 minutes.

2. Meanwhile, in a medium saucepan, combine 4 cups of water with the rice, saffron, and remaining ¼ teaspoon salt. Bring to a boil, reduce the heat to low, cover, and cook until all the water is absorbed, about 10 minutes.

3. Serve the keema over the cooked rice.

Irish Hash

Saint Patrick's Day in Michigan is kind of crazy. For example, one year we were all downtown in shorts enjoying the early, warm spring weather—but the next year we bundled up against a 20°F snowstorm. Luckily, the green beer still flows. St. Paddy's Day is a great reminder that the carefree days of summer are close.

On St. Patrick's Day, I want festive comfort food. This vegan, gluten-free dish works perfectly, and it is so hearty you won't miss the corned beef. I could make it for breakfast too, but then I'd have to give up my green beer. So put on your cutest green outfit and no matter what the weather, enjoy the luck of the Irish! If you like, put an organic, free-range fried egg on top of each serving.

serves 4

2 tablespoons grapeseed oil

2 large baking potatoes, cut into thin matchsticks

½ cup chopped yellow onion

¼ teaspoon sea salt

⅛ teaspoon freshly ground black pepper

1 large leek (white and pale green part only), sliced

1 red bell pepper, cored, seeded, and chopped

2 cups shredded cabbage

2 tablespoons chopped fresh flat-leaf parsley

1. Heat the oil in a large skillet set over medium heat. Add the potatoes, onion, salt, and pepper and cook, stirring frequently, until the potatoes begin to brown, about 7 minutes. Add the leek and red pepper and continue cooking until the potatoes are golden brown and cooked through, about 7 more minutes.
2. Stir in the cabbage and parsley and remove the pan from the heat. Season to taste with salt and pepper. Serve hot.

Vegan Orange Cream Pops

All the credit for this recipe goes to my daughter. She was craving something sweet one night and created this healthy dessert. I was astounded and a bit embarrassed that I didn't think of it. Still, many kudos to her. What fifteen-year-old thinks up something so fresh and delicious as a late-night snack? I am forever amazed at what I learn from my children!

makes 12 orange cream pops

2 cups fresh orange juice

¼ cup fresh lemon juice

3 tablespoons maple syrup

1 (14-ounce) can coconut milk

½ teaspoon vanilla extract

1. In a small bowl, combine the orange juice, lemon juice, and 2 tablespoons of the maple syrup. In a separate bowl, combine the coconut milk, vanilla, and remaining 1 tablespoon maple syrup.

2. Put 1 tablespoon of the coconut milk mixture in the bottom of each of 12 ice-pop molds. Spoon 3 tablespoons of the juice mixture into each, followed by another 1 tablespoon of the coconut milk mixture. Freeze until completely frozen, about 3 hours.

Warm Pear Crumble

Pears are a wonderful winter and early spring fruit. They are widely available this time of year, and their mild sweet taste offers a freshness that's so appealing in the winter months. I especially love combining pear with lemon, because the tart of lemon juice nicely balances the sweet pear, and then adding the ginger gives it just a hint of spiciness. This dish is akin to a summer cobbler with its bubbly sweet fruit and crumbly top, yet so seasonally appropriate.

serves 4 to 6

¼ cup (½ stick) plus 2 teaspoons unsalted butter, chilled and cut into small pieces

¼ cup honey

2 tablespoons tapioca starch

1 tablespoon fresh lemon juice

¾ teaspoon grated fresh ginger

6 firm, ripe Anjou pears, peeled, cored, and coarsely chopped

¼ cup rolled oats

½ cup almond meal

2 tablespoons organic cane sugar

⅛ teaspoon sea salt

1. Preheat the oven to 350°F. Grease an 8-inch square baking dish with 2 teaspoons of the butter and set aside.
2. In a large bowl, combine the honey, tapioca starch, lemon juice, and ginger. Add the pears and toss to coat. Pour the mixture into the prepared baking dish and cover loosely with foil. Bake until hot and bubbly, about 45 minutes.
3. Meanwhile, put the oats in a food processor and process until coarsely ground. Transfer to a medium bowl. Add the almond meal, sugar, and salt. Add the remaining ¼ cup butter and, using a fork, blend in the butter until the mixture is crumbly.
4. Remove the foil from the baking dish and sprinkle the crumble topping over the pears. Return the pan to the oven and cook until the top is golden, 20 to 25 minutes. Let cool for at least 5 minutes before serving.
5. Serve hot, warm, or at room temperature.

april

Egg White Scramble with Curried Goat Cheese and Dandelion Greens

Strawberry Hemp Milk Shake

Salt-Roasted Beets with Watercress, Honey, and Lemon

Arugula Salad with Raspberries, Pecans, and Raspberry Vinaigrette

Egg Noodles with Wild Mushrooms and Spring Greens

Asparagus with Turmeric-Spiced Almonds

Roasted Cauliflower with Quinoa and Cashews

Garlic and Thyme Mashed Potatoes

Lavender-Infused Custard with Honey and Lemon

Angel Food Cake with Tart Raspberry Sauce

April is the ***month of spring*** herbs and local baby greens. The earth itself is turning green again after a long, brown winter, and the greenery spreads to local stores, which burst at the seams with herbs, lettuces, asparagus, garlic, spring onions, and wild mushrooms.

I am truly in awe of how ***the earth provides food***. These days we are socialized into thinking we always have to pay for food, but so many amazing things will sprout from our very own yards if we only plant and wait. This is why I enjoy gardening. Growing a garden is like planting a money tree. It is so worth it to garden even if you start small with just a few herbs, which are practically effortless to maintain and ***yield amazing flavors***, as well as savings. Even if you don't have a yard, you can grow plenty of things in pots on a front porch or in window boxes. It's such a joy to walk outside and go from pot to pot picking a few basil leaves, a few spinach leaves, some thyme, mint, and rosemary, and make a small salad out of this harvest. There is nothing as satisfying, nutritious, and delicious as that! Whatever you're inspired to do, ***growing your own food is an activity*** that will give you immense satisfaction.

APRIL

Here is a sample menu I've put together with
a variety of recipes for this month.

breakfast

Egg White Scramble with Curried Goat Cheese and Dandelion Greens

•

lunch

Egg Noodles with Wild Mushrooms and Spring Greens

•

midday snack

Lavender-Infused Custard with Honey and Lemon

•

dinner

Roasted Cauliflower with Quinoa and Cashews

•

dessert

Angel Food Cake with Tart Raspberry Sauce

Egg White Scramble *with* Curried Goat Cheese *and* Dandelion Greens

The next time you are at the grocery store, spend some extra time looking at the interesting greens. Pick a few that you have never tried before. If you have to, munch on a leaf or two in the store to see what they taste like. Greens are perhaps the healthiest food on earth, as they provide our bodies with nutrients unmatched in variety and amount. People think they taste bad, but while some types are strong or bitter, most are mild. Dandelion greens are a great complement to this dish because of their zingy flavor. Like most greens, they deliver powerful antioxidants, calcium, iron, potassium, and vitamins A, C, and K. Sometimes in this recipe I use spinach or arugula greens instead of dandelion greens, all of which are available at my local grocery store.

serves 4

4 ounces goat cheese (local, if possible)

¼ teaspoon curry powder

⅛ teaspoon sea salt

Pinch of turmeric

1 bunch dandelion greens, coarsely chopped

1 tablespoon grapeseed oil

12 large egg whites, lightly beaten

1. In a small bowl, combine the goat cheese, curry powder, salt, and turmeric. Set aside.
2. Place dandelion greens on individual serving plates and set aside.
3. Heat the oil in a large nonstick skillet set over medium-high heat. Add the egg whites and cook, stirring constantly, scraping the bottom of the pan with a heatproof spatula, until just cooked through, about 4 minutes.
4. Spoon the eggs over the dandelion greens, top with the goat cheese mixture, and serve immediately.

tip *local creameries and community supported agriculture*

More and more, local creameries and Community Supported Agriculture (CSA) groups are popping up all over the country. People are more interested in buying locally produced items because there is a growing distrust of large food companies as well as a desire to support local farms. CSA farms grow seasonal produce and sell this produce directly to individuals.

In the small town of Fennville, Michigan, near where we live, there is a place called Evergreen Lane Farm & Creamery. Several years ago a family purchased this farm and converted it to an organic apple orchard, and they also started a creamery with a small herd of goats. Visiting Evergreen Lane with my children teaches them the connection between what we eat and the land that produces it. The experience of having them pet the goats, see the babies, and pick apples from the orchard and later cook with them at home is priceless. Nothing beats the flavor of seasonal, fresh, and local ingredients. To find local farms and CSAs near you, visit www.localharvest.org.

Strawberry Hemp Milk Shake

Have you ever read the ingredients on the back of a conventional store-bought strawberry milk container? It will blow your mind. The amount of manufactured ingredients that go into conventional strawberry milk is crazy! Making your own is easy and something you can do in less than 10 minutes. This shake truly does a body good!

I love making this with raw hemp hearts because of all the nutritional benefits. It is a complete vegan protein that is rich in omega-3 fats and has an abundance of vitamins and minerals, including calcium, iron, vitamins A and D, and several B vitamins. Hemp milk has a distinct taste, and I like to flavor it, as I've done here. Unlike other nut milks, it does not need to be strained because the entire heart blends into a smooth consistency. You can find hemp hearts at your local natural food store or online.

serves 4

2 cups strawberries, hulled
½ cup hemp hearts
2 cups cold filtered water
½ cup fresh orange juice
1 tablespoon maple syrup
Pinch of sea salt

In a blender or Vitamix, combine the strawberries, hemp, water, orange juice, maple syrup, and salt. Blend on high until smooth, 3 to 4 minutes. Refrigerate and serve chilled. The shake will keep in an airtight container in the refrigerator for up to 3 days.

Salt-Roasted Beets *with* Watercress, Honey, *and* Lemon

Beets are still widely available this time of year and I always choose a variety if the store carries them. Salt-roasting beets locks in flavor and, to me, is a foolproof way to get tender and tasty root vegetables every time. But be forewarned that beets can make quite a mess! You can always wear gloves to keep your hands from getting too red, but my theory is that what's good for the body is good for the skin, which is why whenever I work with fruits and vegetables, I rub the juices into my skin. And even though I try to keep a vegan diet, I am a firm believer in the power of honey. As nature's most natural sweetener, honey has strong antimicrobial benefits and protective antioxidants as well as an array of vitamins, minerals, fatty acids, and amino acids.

serves 4

3 medium beets with greens

½ cup coarse or kosher salt

3 medium carrots, quartered

1 tablespoon honey

1 tablespoon fresh lemon juice

2 tablespoons olive oil

⅛ teaspoon sea salt

Pinch of freshly ground black pepper

3 cups loosely packed watercress

1. Preheat the oven to 400°F.
2. Trim the root end off the beets. Cut off the greens, trim off and discard the stems, and chop the greens. Put the greens in a bowl, cover, and refrigerate.
3. Pour the salt onto a small rimmed baking sheet. Arrange the beets on top of the salt.
4. Roast the beets for 55 minutes. Add the carrots to the pan, nestled into the salt next to the beets, and roast until the vegetables are tender, about 35 minutes. Remove the pan from the oven and let cool.
5. When the beets are cool enough to handle, peel the skins and discard. Slice the beets and carrots ¼ inch thick.
6. In a large bowl, whisk together the honey, lemon juice, olive oil, salt, and pepper. Add the watercress, reserved beet greens, and carrots, and toss to coat. Divide among 4 plates and top with the sliced beets. Serve.

Arugula Salad *with* Raspberries, Pecans, *and* Raspberry Vinaigrette

One of my constant mottos in life is "less is more." Thinking "less" has saved me time, money, and anxiety: less shampoo, less makeup, less clothes, less furniture, less stuff. People respond to simple, we understand simple. We like things that are uncomplicated.

One of the most fun aspects of cooking for me is creating the biggest flavor with the simplest ingredients. Luckily, Mother Nature makes this easy because the world is filled with amazing foods that burst with flavor. Raspberries are a perfect example. Has the human race ever created something that beats the raspberry in taste? I think not! I especially love pairing them with a nut like pecans because the rich and savory flavor from the nuts is a perfect complement to the sweet raspberries.

serves 4

1 (5-ounce) package arugula or baby spinach

½ cup raspberries

½ cup pecan pieces

1 small red onion, thinly sliced

¼ teaspoon turmeric

Raspberry Vinaigrette (recipe follows)

1. Put the arugula in a medium bowl. Add the raspberries, pecan pieces, and onion. Sprinkle with the turmeric.
2. To serve, drizzle with the dressing and toss gently.

raspberry vinaigrette

½ cup fresh raspberries

¼ cup extra-virgin olive oil

2 tablespoons fresh lemon juice

1 tablespoon honey

Salt and freshly ground black pepper

In a blender, combine the raspberries, olive oil, lemon juice, and honey and purée until smooth. Season to taste with salt and pepper. The vinaigrette will keep in an airtight container in the refrigerator for up to a week. ***makes ¾ cup***

Egg Noodles *with* Wild Mushrooms *and* Spring Greens

April is the month when you may start to find local greens and wild mushrooms at your neighborhood farmer's market or natural food store. It is always surprising to me how early in the season delicate lettuces and greens can be grown. Our local CSA starts to deliver more and more young tender spring greens to our natural food store, and this is the perfect time to enjoy them in your recipes. If you can find wild mushrooms, they'll make this dish superb!

serves 4

1 (12-ounce) package extra-wide egg noodles

1 teaspoon sea salt, plus more to taste

5 ounces mixed spring greens (about 2 cups)

2 tablespoons olive oil, plus more for drizzling

2 tablespoons all-purpose flour

3 cups sliced wild mushrooms

1 large onion, thinly sliced

1 cup vegetable broth, homemade (see Tip, page 183) or store-bought

½ cup dry white wine

Freshly ground black pepper

½ cup shaved Parmesan cheese (optional)

1. In a medium pot, bring 6 cups of water to a boil over high heat. Add the egg noodles and 1 teaspoon salt, reduce the heat to keep the water at a low boil, and cook until the noodles are done, about 10 minutes (or cook according to the package directions). Drain the noodles and transfer to a large serving bowl. Stir in the greens. Cover and let sit for 2 minutes.

2. Meanwhile, in a large skillet set over medium-low heat, combine the olive oil, flour, mushrooms, and onion. Cook, stirring, until the mushrooms and onion are soft and lightly browned, about 10 minutes. Slowly add the vegetable broth and white wine and cook, stirring constantly, until the mixture begins to thicken, 3 to 4 minutes. Season with salt and pepper, and remove the pan from the heat.

3. Pour the mushroom mixture over the noodles and greens and toss to coat. Drizzle with olive oil and top with the shaved Parmesan.

tip *natural pest deterrents*

It is that time of year again when we all come out of hibernation here in the North; even the bugs enjoy the arrival of warmer weather and will make themselves feel at home in all your spaces. But there are some natural products you can use that will discourage pests in the first place.

- CEDAR: It naturally repels almost all insects and has a wonderful aroma. Spread cedar chips around plants in the yard and place them in cupboards and closets to deter bugs.
- MINT: To make a bug repellent, grind fresh mint leaves into a paste (or opt for peppermint or spearmint oil), mix with some water, and spray around doors and windows that bugs frequent.
- BASIL, SAGE, AND ROSEMARY: The scent of these herbs repels flies and mosquitoes.
- MARIGOLDS: Plant these around your yard to deter bugs.
- PURPLE MARTIN BIRDHOUSE OR A BAT HOUSE: Draw these birds and bats into your yard to eat thousands of mosquitoes a day!
- HOT WATER AND STEAM: Kill insects and dust mites instantly in clothes and furniture.
- FOOD-GRADE DIATOMACEOUS EARTH: If you have a really tough problem, like an ant infestation or a flea outbreak, use this natural powder to kill all sorts of insects.

Asparagus *with* Turmeric-Spiced Almonds

Turmeric is one of the world's healthiest spices and has a neutral enough flavor that you can sprinkle it on just about anything. It is a spice that has been used in Indian and Asian cuisines for centuries, and recent studies have shown it to be effective in reducing inflammation, which is the precursor of many diseases. Turmeric is very high in antioxidants, ranking sixth among all spices and eighth among all foods. Its mildly bitter flavor combines wonderfully with agave and lemon juice. This dish is so hearty and beautiful that it can be served as a main course for lunch with crusty bread and olive oil and some cut-up fruit.

serves 4 to 5

1 tablespoon grapeseed oil, plus more for pan

1 tablespoon agave nectar

⅛ teaspoon turmeric

¼ teaspoon sea salt

Pinch of ground cumin

⅓ cup sliced almonds

1 pound asparagus, tough stems removed and cut into 3-inch pieces

1 tablespoon fresh lemon juice

1. Preheat the oven to 325°F. Grease a baking sheet with oil and set aside.
2. In a small bowl, combine the agave, turmeric, salt, and cumin. Add the almonds and stir gently to coat. Spread the almonds on the prepared baking sheet and bake until lightly golden, about 7 minutes. Set aside.
3. Heat the oil in a large heavy skillet set over medium heat. Add the asparagus and cook, stirring frequently, until just tender, about 5 minutes. Transfer the asparagus to a serving dish. Sprinkle with the lemon juice and then the almond mixture. Serve.

Roasted Cauliflower *with* Quinoa *and* Cashews

Quinoa is an ancient grain with a high amount of protein. The term *ancient grain* refers to a grain that has been grown and unaltered for thousands of years. Grains like chia, hemp, amaranth, and flax were often used as staple nutrients by ancient civilizations. Quinoa is especially valuable because it is a complete vegan protein, which means that it provides all of the amino acids your body needs. Quinoa is also high in antioxidants and fiber.

I find that cooking with quinoa takes a bit of practice, because although it is mild in flavor, some people do not care for the taste and texture. It is important to pair quinoa with the right flavors and textures to create a satisfying meal.

serves 6

2 cups filtered water

1 cup tricolor quinoa, rinsed and drained

1 head cauliflower, cut into florets

2 cups halved cherry or grape tomatoes

2 tablespoons grapeseed oil

½ teaspoon ground cumin

Sea salt and freshly ground black pepper

½ cup roasted unsalted cashews

¼ cup chopped fresh chives

1. In a small saucepan set over high heat, combine the water and quinoa. Bring to a boil, reduce the heat to low, cover, and cook until the water is absorbed, about 20 minutes. Remove the pan from the heat and set aside.
2. Preheat the oven to 425°F.
3. Put the cauliflower and tomatoes on a large rimmed baking sheet and drizzle with the oil. Sprinkle with the cumin, season with salt and pepper, and toss well.
4. Roast for 10 minutes. Stir in the cashews and continue roasting until the cauliflower is golden brown and just tender, about 10 minutes.
5. Transfer the roasted vegetables and cashews to a large bowl. Toss with the chives and cooked quinoa. Season to taste with salt and pepper. Serve hot, at room temperature, or chilled.

tip *natural spring cleaning*

Like everything else, the more I clean, the better I get at it—and the more I save time and money. I also want my house to be a toxin-free zone, so I transitioned to making my own natural cleaning products. It's amazing what can be done with just baking soda and vinegar. Baking soda is a wonderful natural scrub for sinks, tubs, and toilets. Vinegar is a natural deodorizer, and its mild acidity breaks down dirt and germs. I often add peppermint oil to my cleaning solutions, too, because it has antimicrobial qualities and smells amazing. Here are my three staples for cleaning.

SCRUB: Make a paste with baking soda and water. Add a few drops of peppermint oil.

GLASS AND COUNTER: Mix equal parts white vinegar and water.

FLOOR CLEANER: Mix ½ cup of white vinegar with 1 gallon of very hot water.

Garlic *and* Thyme Mashed Potatoes

Mashed potatoes in my opinion are one of life's simple pleasures. When made with nondairy milk and paired with nutrition powerhouses like garlic and thyme, they become a healthy dish rather than an indulgence. I always encourage people to find ways to make their favorite dishes healthier instead of just walking away from them. For many recipes, that means a compromise on ingredients, finding a balance that gives great taste along with great health. That is why I still sometimes use real butter in this recipe. It is also great made completely vegan, but my theory is that life is about meeting in the middle—and sometimes I just want some butter.

serves 6

3 garlic cloves

8 medium russet potatoes, peeled and quartered

2 teaspoons sea salt

1½ to 2 cups unsweetened almond milk, homemade (page 34) or store-bought

6 tablespoons salted butter or vegan buttery spread

2 tablespoons fresh thyme leaves

Freshly ground black pepper

1. Preheat the oven to 350°F.
2. Wrap the unpeeled garlic cloves in aluminum foil and roast until soft, about 30 minutes. Remove the garlic from the oven and let cool.
3. Meanwhile, put the potatoes in a large pot with enough water to cover and add the salt. Bring to a boil over high heat and cook until the potatoes are soft, about 15 minutes. Drain the potatoes and return them to the pot.
4. When the garlic is cool enough to handle, peel and chop the cloves. Add the garlic, almond milk, and butter to the potatoes. Mash well with a potato masher until the desired consistency is reached. Stir in the thyme, season to taste with pepper, and serve warm.

Lavender-Infused Custard *with* Honey *and* Lemon

When I was growing up, my mom used to make custard for dessert sometimes. I was always a little tentative and never a huge fan because it tasted so eggy. One of the most amazing discoveries for me is using tofu to thicken and in a way mimic eggs and dairy like heavy cream in dessert recipes, as in this custard. I actually love how it tastes now, and I've come up with of all sorts of yummy creamy desserts that are much healthier for me (see my tip on cooking with tofu on page 137). My version of my mom's custard is thick and creamy with lavender from the garden (or your local spice shop), honey, and lemon.

serves 4

¼ cup almond milk, homemade (page 34) or store-bought

1½ teaspoons lavender, plus more for garnish

1 (12-ounce) package firm tofu

3 tablespoons honey

1 teaspoon fresh lemon juice

1. In a small saucepan set over medium-low heat, combine the almond milk and lavender. Bring the mixture to a boil and immediately remove the pan from the heat. Let steep for 5 minutes. Pour through a strainer into a small bowl and set aside.
2. In the bowl of a food processor, combine the tofu, honey, and lemon juice. Process until the mixture is very smooth. Add the lavender almond milk and pulse until combined.
3. Pour the mixture into 4 custard cups or ramekins. Cover and refrigerate until set, at least 2 hours or overnight.
4. Garnish with a very light sprinkling of lavender before serving.

Angel Food Cake *with* Tart Raspberry Sauce

The last time I made this cake, my fifteen-year-old looked at me as she was devouring a piece and asked, "Is this cake good for you, Mom?" I didn't hesitate to say "yes!" With no oils, minimal sugar, and great extras like lemon zest, raspberries, and fresh squeezed lemon juice, this cake is way too good for you to taste this delicious. It is always a hit at a gathering, and never sits on the counter long at home. It is perfect for an afternoon snack with a cup of green tea, and I won't tell anyone if you eat a piece for breakfast, too!

makes one 10-inch cake

CAKE

1¼ cups organic confectioners' sugar

1 cup organic cake flour

¼ teaspoon sea salt

9 large egg whites

1½ teaspoons cream of tartar

1 cup organic cane sugar, blended (see page 9)

2 teaspoons vanilla extract

Grated zest of 2 lemons

SAUCE

¼ cup fresh lemon juice

¼ cup agave nectar

2 teaspoons vanilla extract

2 cups raspberries

1. Preheat the oven to 350°F.
2. For the cake, in a medium bowl, whisk together the confectioners' sugar, flour, and salt.
3. In the bowl of an electric mixer fitted with the whisk attachment, beat the egg whites on medium speed until foamy, about 1 minute. Sprinkle in the cream of tartar and beat at medium-high speed until soft peaks form, about 2 minutes. Sprinkle in the cane sugar and beat at high speed until the egg whites are thick and shiny, about 3 minutes. Add the vanilla and lemon zest and beat just to combine.
4. Gradually sift the flour mixture into the egg whites, folding in using a rubber spatula. Spoon the batter into a nonstick 10-inch tube pan with a removable bottom.
5. Bake until the cake is golden, about 50 minutes. Invert the tube pan onto the neck of a wine bottle or metal funnel. Let cool completely, about 1 hour.

6. Tap on the bottom of the pan to loosen the cake and carefully turn the cake out onto a cake plate.

7. For the sauce, in a small saucepan set over high heat, combine the lemon juice, agave, and vanilla. Bring to a boil. Add half of the raspberries and mash them into the liquid with a large spoon. Bring the mixture back to a boil, reduce the heat to low, and cook until the mixture thickens, about 2 minutes. Remove the pan from the heat. Stir in the remaining half of the berries and let cool.

8. To serve, spoon the sauce over slices of cake.

may

Rhubarb Breakfast Crisp

Almond Butter and
Cacao Nib Smoothie

Cheddar Artichoke Dip

Linguine with Tomatoes
and Avocado Pesto

Watercress, Cucumber,
and Toasted Pecan Salad

Hummus, Tomato, and Caper
Bruschetta

Asparagus Risotto

Garlic and Fennel–Stuffed
Portobello Mushrooms

Mother's Day Strawberry,
Mango, and Coconut Mousse

Corn Bread Pudding
with Fennel

Each May, Holland, Michigan, hosts one of the largest festivals in the nation: ***Tulip Time.*** The weeklong festival boasts hundreds of thousands of tulips planted throughout our beautiful little city, several parades and events, and our famous Dutch Dancers. The dance teams perform throughout the week in long, seemingly endless lines of flowing colors. And the musicians in our hometown Holland High School Marching Band march in traditional wooden shoes.

Having a ***festival in Michigan*** during the month of May is pretty daring because you never know what the weather will bring. Occasionally, we have a "stem fest" because the weather has been so hot that all the tulips have bloomed and died before the festival.

Other years, it's so cold that the tulips are only buds. But ***sometimes we have*** that perfect year with ***pristine weather*** and the tulips are in full bloom. Holland is, at that time, the most beautiful place on earth.

May also brings the exciting seasonal opening of the farmer's market. Surrounding the town is a ***strong agricultural community*** that is incredibly bountiful during the summer and fall.

MAY

Here is a sample menu I've put together with a variety of recipes for this month.

breakfast

Rhubarb Breakfast Crisp

•

lunch

Linguine with Tomatoes and Avocado Pesto

•

midday snack

Corn Bread Pudding with Fennel

•

dinner

Garlic and Fennel–Stuffed Portobello Mushrooms

•

dessert

Mother's Day Strawberry, Mango, and Coconut Mousse

Rhubarb Breakfast Crisp

One fruit that seems to be synonymous with being Dutch and living in a northern climate is rhubarb. Everyone I know has a grandma that makes the *best* rhubarb pie. Everyone I know has a recipe for a killer rhubarb sauce, soup, or stew. Rhubarb is cheap, delicious, nutritious, and almost impossible not to grow around here. Try getting rid of an established rhubarb plant. I guarantee you will come close to breaking your shovel.

As with asparagus, the first shoots of rhubarb are a telltale sign of spring and a welcome addition to your spring palate. Combining rhubarb with oats, nuts, and brown sugar makes this breakfast decadent yet healthy and functional.

serves 4 to 6

Grapeseed oil, for pan

½ cup plus ⅓ cup unsweetened applesauce

⅔ cup maple syrup

1 teaspoon fresh lemon juice

1½ tablespoons tapioca starch

½ teaspoon ground cinnamon

6 rhubarb stalks, sliced ¼ inch thick

2 Fuji or Rome apples, peeled, cored, and chopped

1 cup organic granola, homemade (page 210) or store-bought

1. Preheat the oven to 350°F. Grease a 9-inch pie dish with grapeseed oil and set aside.
2. In a large bowl, combine ½ cup of the applesauce, the maple syrup, lemon juice, tapioca starch, and cinnamon. Add the rhubarb and apples, and toss well. Transfer to the prepared pie dish, cover loosely with foil, and put the pie dish on a baking sheet.
3. Bake until bubbly, 30 to 35 minutes.
4. Meanwhile, combine the granola and remaining ⅓ cup applesauce in a small bowl. Remove the foil from the pie dish and sprinkle the granola mixture over the top of the rhubarb. Return to the oven and cook, uncovered, until the topping is lightly golden, about 12 minutes.
5. Let cool for at least 5 minutes before serving. Serve hot, warm, or at room temperature.

Almond Butter *and* Cacao Nib Smoothie

I have two wonderful teenage daughters whose bright personalities and motivated spirits inspire me daily, but getting them to eat breakfast can be a challenge! Sleep, hair, and makeup take precedence over calories, something I understand all too well. Getting them out the door with a nutritious start to the day is not an easy task. This is why morning smoothies are a lifesaver for me. It's effortless to straighten your hair and drink a smoothie at the same time.

Almond butter with almond milk and fruit creates a dessert-like protein-rich start to their day that fills them up and makes me feel like I did my mom job. Add a handful of raspberries, strawberries, or frozen peaches to this recipe, if you want.

serves 2

1½ cups almond milk, homemade (page 34) or store-bought

1 tablespoon maple syrup

1 teaspoon vanilla

1 tablespoon coconut oil

3 medium bananas, frozen

¼ cup almond butter

2 tablespoons cacao nibs, plus more for garnish

In a blender, combine the almond milk, maple syrup, vanilla, coconut oil, bananas, almond butter, and cacao nibs and purée until smooth. Pour into glasses and garnish with additional cacao nibs. Serve immediately.

tip detoxifying foods

Detox is all the rage. People spend hundreds of dollars on special concoctions to rid their bodies of evil toxins. I'm not a huge fan of juice cleanses because I think they are unnatural and potentially dangerous if they do not provide the right amount of vitamins and minerals. I do, however, believe in continuous detoxing by paying attention to your diet. Eating a variety of whole, fresh produce helps your body detox on a daily basis. Here are my favorite detoxifying foods:

Lemons **Broccoli** **Artichokes**
Kale **Turmeric** **Almonds**

Cheddar Artichoke Dip

I am a child of the 1980s who grew up in a Dutch family mainly in small Dutch communities. Many of the recipes I grew up on were filled with all things creamy—mayonnaise, sour cream, and whipped cream—and Jell-O salads with all of the above ingredients were served at almost every potluck.

When you grow up with certain foods it's hard to leave them behind, but that's why creating better versions of them is so much fun! This is my version of the mayonnaise- and sour cream–filled artichoke dip that I grew up with. What I adore about this dish is the addition of red peppers and scallions, which add flavor and tons of healthy nutrients. I use local, organic Cheddar and organic cottage cheese, too. It ends up being rich and delicious but with great healthy benefits.

serves 8 to 10

1 (14-ounce) can artichoke hearts in water, drained and coarsely chopped

1 (16-ounce) container cottage cheese

¾ cup coarsely chopped roasted or fresh red bell pepper

½ teaspoon sea salt

8 ounces shredded Cheddar cheese (2 cups)

¼ cup chopped fresh chives

1. Preheat the oven to 350°F. Grease a 1-quart casserole dish or soufflé dish and set aside.
2. Wrap the artichoke hearts in several layers of paper towels and press gently to remove excess moisture. Set aside.
3. In the bowl of a food processor, combine the cottage cheese, bell pepper, and salt and purée until smooth and creamy. Add the artichoke hearts and 1½ cups of the Cheddar cheese, and pulse until the artichokes are finely chopped. Add the chives and pulse once or twice to combine. Spoon the mixture into the prepared casserole dish and sprinkle with the remaining ½ cup Cheddar cheese.
4. Bake until heated through and the cheese on top begins to brown, about 20 minutes. Serve hot or warm.

Linguine *with* Tomatoes *and* Avocado Pesto

Pesto is traditionally an Italian sauce made with pine nuts, basil, Parmesan, and olive oil. I like to put a twist on it by using avocado oil and adding a full avocado, the richness of which negates the necessity for cheese.

Tomato sauces are great, but sometimes you need something smooth and rich like a pesto brings. Most people use a food processor for pesto. It works great when I'm short on time, but if I can, I like to chop my ingredients by hand. I prefer to have a chunky pesto, and the rhythmic motions of preparing the pesto by hand are calming and peaceful to me. I love this pesto mixed into linguine and topped with fresh chopped tomatoes from the garden, or I use it as a sandwich spread with tomatoes, cucumbers, and greens.

serves 6

1 (12-ounce) package linguine

Avocado Pesto (recipe follows)

2 tomatoes, cored and chopped

Cook the linguine according to the package instructions. Drain and toss into a serving bowl. Add the pesto and toss well. Top with the tomatoes. Serve warm or at room temperature.

avocado pesto

2 cups fresh basil leaves, finely chopped

1 cup pine nuts, crushed

1 whole avocado, peeled, pitted, and chopped

¼ cup avocado oil or olive oil

⅛ teaspoon sea salt

Freshly ground black pepper

In a medium bowl, combine the basil, pine nuts, avocado, and oil. Mash the ingredients together with a potato masher until well blended. Alternatively, pulse the ingredients in a food processor until smooth, about 30 seconds. Add the salt and season to taste with pepper. ***makes about 1½ cups***

Watercress, Cucumber, *and* Toasted Pecan Salad

It's sometimes hard for me to write a specific recipe for a salad because so often the salad turns out to be a big bowl of whatever is in my fridge. My good friend Kristin makes a salad almost daily and calls it her "big bowl of happy." When creating a recipe, add ingredients that you think will blend well. Watercress, which is a cruciferous vegetable, is an excellent source of vitamins C, K, and A. It is incredibly high in antioxidants and has remarkable anticancer properties. I find it very similar to arugula in taste, so I often interchange the two greens. If you have some pickled green beans (page 53) sitting on your counter, they make a wonderful addition to this salad.

serves 4

1 tablespoon grapeseed oil

1 tablespoon packed organic dark brown sugar

¼ teaspoon ground ginger

½ cup coarsely chopped pecans

4 teaspoons rice vinegar

¼ cup extra-virgin olive oil

1 teaspoon peeled and grated fresh ginger

1 cucumber, thinly sliced

1 bunch watercress (about 2 cups loosely packed)

1 mango, peeled, pitted, and cut into cubes

1. Preheat the oven to 350°F. Line a baking sheet with parchment paper.
2. In a small bowl, combine the grapeseed oil, sugar, and ground ginger. Add the pecans and stir well. Spread the pecans on the prepared baking sheet and bake until they are aromatic, about 7 minutes. Set aside to cool.
3. In a large bowl, whisk together the vinegar, olive oil, and fresh ginger. Add the cucumber, watercress, and mango, and toss well. Sprinkle with the spiced pecans and serve immediately.

Hummus, Tomato, *and* Caper Bruschetta

There are endless possibilities when it comes to creating a bruschetta. Often on a warm night I make several varieties of it for dinner. I always make my own toasts with sliced organic baguettes, olive oil, and garlic salt. Hummus is a staple in our house. It's easy to make, filling, delicious, and healthy. Spreading hummus on the toasts and adding salty capers, fresh tomatoes, and some pepper makes for a hearty appetizer, or even a perfect main course paired with a light soup or salad. If you want to make your own hummus, use my recipe on page 37.

serves 6

1 baguette, cut into 24 rounds

3 tablespoons olive oil

Garlic salt

1 cup chopped tomatoes

2 tablespoons finely chopped onion

2 tablespoons capers

1 cup hummus

Freshly ground black pepper

1. Preheat the oven to 350°F.
2. Arrange the baguette slices on a baking sheet and brush them with 2 tablespoons of the olive oil. Sprinkle with the garlic salt and bake until toasted, about 10 minutes. Let cool.
3. In a bowl, combine the remaining 1 tablespoon olive oil, tomatoes, onion, and capers.
4. To serve, spread each toast with the hummus and top with the tomato-caper mixture. Season each with pepper.

Asparagus Risotto

One of the first houses I owned had this big bushy plant growing randomly in the backyard. I could not for the life of me figure out what it was, and it was so ugly that I almost dug it out. But I thought I should wait at least a year to see what the plant did. The next spring, to my delight, out of the ground sprouted shoot after shoot of baby asparagus. A full-grown asparagus plant looks nothing like what we eat. We eat only the young shoots, and the tip is the bud that will eventually become feathery leaves.

I adore a fresh, light asparagus risotto like this one. Often I use half the cheese and a cup of almond milk or other nut milk in place of a cup of broth, to keep it lower in dairy yet still creamy and delicious.

serves 4

6 cups vegetable broth, homemade (see Tip, page 183) or store-bought

2 tablespoons grapeseed oil

½ cup finely chopped yellow onion

2 cups Arborio rice

1 cup dry white wine

1½ teaspoons sea salt

½ teaspoon freshly ground black pepper

20 medium asparagus stalks, trimmed and cut into 1-inch pieces

½ cup grated Parmesan cheese (optional)

2 tablespoons chopped fresh chives

1. In a medium saucepan set over medium heat, bring the broth to a simmer. Reduce the heat to low and keep the broth at a low simmer.
2. Heat the oil in a large skillet set over medium heat. Add the onion and cook, stirring frequently, until lightly golden, about 6 minutes. Add the rice and cook, stirring, until it starts to smell toasted, about 2 minutes. Add the wine, salt, and pepper and cook, stirring constantly, until most of the wine has been absorbed, about 2 minutes. Reduce the heat to medium-low. Slowly add 1 cup of the hot broth and cook, stirring constantly, until nearly all of the broth has been absorbed, about 2 minutes. Repeat the addition of broth 3 times. Stir in the asparagus along with the next 1 cup of broth and cook, stirring constantly, until almost absorbed, about 2 minutes each time. Keep adding broth, stirring between additions, until the risotto is creamy and the rice is just cooked through, about 5 more minutes.
3. Remove the pan from the heat, stir in the cheese and chives, and serve hot.

tip *sea salt versus table salt*

I have to admit, I am much more of a salt girl than a sugar girl. Salt is a wonderful ingredient that when used in moderation can enhance sweet and savory dishes alike. However, I think it is important to understand that there is a better choice when it comes to salt. Normal table salt typically comes from underground salt deposits. It is highly processed at temperatures over 1000°F and bleached to remove additional minerals and create a pure-looking, white product. The salt is then combined with anticaking chemicals to give it a longer shelf life. Most table salt has iodine added as well, for nutritional reasons.

Sea salt is an unprocessed, unrefined salt that comes from seawater that is collected and evaporated down to salt crystals. These crystals contain many beneficial trace minerals, including calcium, iodine, magnesium, iron, potassium, and zinc, which are easily absorbed and utilized by our bodies. When you taste table salt and sea salt side by side, the flavor difference is enormous, as the natural product is more interesting. You will wonder why you haven't switched earlier.

Garlic *and* Fennel–Stuffed Portobello Mushrooms

Portobello mushrooms have a wonderful rich, meaty flavor that I like to enhance. Whenever I cook them, I scoop out the gills, which are the brown folds underneath the caps. They are fully edible but I dispose of them because they often release liquid when cooked that can make your dish soggy. They're simple to remove, and your recipe will turn out better.

I have always loved stuffed mushrooms. This hearty recipe is a vegan comfort food that your entire family will love! And don't discard the tops of the fennel, as they make a pretty garnish.

serves 4

1 tablespoon grapeseed oil, plus more for pan

4 large (4-inch) or 8 medium (3-inch) portobello mushrooms

⅓ cup finely chopped yellow onion

½ cup grated carrot

½ cup finely chopped fennel bulb

3 tablespoons chopped fennel fronds

1½ teaspoons minced garlic

½ teaspoon sea salt

¼ teaspoon freshly ground black pepper

1 cup panko bread crumbs

1. Preheat the oven to 400°F. Grease a small baking sheet with grapeseed oil.
2. Remove the stems from the mushrooms and chop the stems, leaving the caps whole. Scoop the gills out of the mushroom caps and discard. Put the mushroom caps top-side down on the prepared baking sheet.
3. Heat the grapeseed oil in a medium skillet set over medium-high heat. Add the chopped mushroom stems, onion, carrot, fennel bulb, fennel fronds, garlic, salt, and pepper. Cook, stirring frequently, until softened, about 5 minutes. Remove the pan from the heat and add the bread crumbs. Fill the mushroom caps with the bread-crumb mixture and arrange them on the prepared baking sheet.
4. Bake until golden brown, about 13 minutes. Serve hot or at room temperature.

Mother's Day Strawberry, Mango, *and* Coconut Mousse

On this special day, I definitely take the time to let my mother, grandmother, and mother-in-law know how much they mean to me and how much I appreciate them, and if there are activities we can all do together that we love, it's even better! Spending Mother's Day indulging in my family is a huge blessing to me.

Although this is an easy and lovely recipe that is decadent and melts in your mouth, you are not allowed to make it on Mother's Day. It is a fantastic recipe to give to your kids and/or spouse to make for you because it is so easy. The only potential problem is that they might eat most of it before you see it!

serves 6

1 (1-pound) package silken tofu

1 mango, peeled, pitted, and chopped

¾ cup shredded unsweetened coconut

3 tablespoons agave nectar

½ teaspoon vanilla extract

½ teaspoon fresh lemon juice

1 cup chopped strawberries

6 strawberries, sliced, for garnish

1. In the bowl of a food processor, combine the tofu, mango, ½ cup of the coconut, the agave, vanilla, and lemon juice. Blend until smooth. Transfer to a bowl and gently stir in the chopped strawberries.
2. Spoon the mixture into ramekins or dessert cups and chill for at least 20 minutes.
3. To serve, garnish with the sliced strawberries and remaining ¼ cup coconut.

Corn Bread Pudding *with* Fennel

Maybe it's the Midwestern girl in me, but I love corn in any way, shape, or form. I always eat organic, non-GMO corn because this crop is one of the most highly genetically modified ones in this country. Pairing corn with the sweet licorice-like taste of the fennel is fantastic. Eat it with or without a drizzle of agave, depending on how sweet you like it. Save the egg whites in this dish to use in the Angel Food Cake with Tart Raspberry Sauce (page 80) or Egg White Scramble with Curried Goat Cheese and Dandelion Greens (page 68).

makes one 8-inch cake

Grapeseed oil, for pan

5 large egg yolks

¾ cup organic cane sugar

2½ cups almond milk, homemade (page 34) or store-bought

¼ teaspoon sea salt

⅔ cup coarse organic cornmeal

1 teaspoon crushed fennel seeds

¼ cup agave nectar (optional)

1. Preheat the oven to 350°F. Grease an 8-inch cake pan with grapeseed oil and set aside.
2. In a large bowl, whisk together the egg yolks and sugar.
3. In a medium saucepan set over medium-high heat, bring the almond milk to a boil. Remove the pan from the heat and gradually whisk the hot milk into the egg yolk mixture. Pour the mixture back into the saucepan and whisk in the salt and cornmeal. Set the pan over medium heat and cook, whisking constantly, until the mixture begins to bubble and thicken, 5 to 6 minutes. Pour the polenta into the prepared pan and sprinkle with the fennel seeds.
4. Bake until golden brown, 40 to 45 minutes. Let cool for at least 30 minutes before drizzling with the agave and serving.

tip aromatherapy

Which smells evoke emotion in you—the scent of a pie baking, the way the air smells after a rain, or the smell of a horse barn, a lake, or fresh coffee? We can use positive emotional connections to smells to our benefit. Certain smell-emotion links are universal, such as lavender's ability to soothe and citrus's ability to boost your mood and even relieve headaches.

This is the idea behind aromatherapy, a practice where people use scents to enhance their moods and stimulate areas of the brain responsible for healing and pain relief. Essential oils are concentrated oils from flowers, leaves, stems, and other plant parts. They often have very strong scents and are used in aromatherapy to relieve stress and create positive feelings. The most commonly used essential oils and their benefits are:

- JASMINE: enhances libido and reduces tension and stress
- LAVENDER: relaxes, calms, and soothes the mind
- PEPPERMINT: enhances mental alertness
- LEMON: enhances mood and relieves headaches
- EUCALYPTUS: fights migraines and soothes aching bodies
- ROSEMARY: stimulates the brain and focuses the mind
- GRAPEFRUIT: energizes

june

Raw Strawberry Jam

Pineapple Sweet Bread

Hummus Pizza with Arugula and Wild Mushrooms

Roasted Broccoli and Hazelnuts

Pineapple Cucumber Gazpacho

Veggie "Sushi" Roll

Fava Bean and Corn Salad

Quinoa with Leeks, Apricots, and Toasted Pecans

Green Chile Enchiladas with Avocado Sauce

Roasted Red Peppers with Goat Cheese

Homemade Lemonade

Strawberry Ice Cream Pie

There is something about ***June*** that ***symbolizes freedom***—it's the end of school and the ***beginning of summer!*** Even though I'm not in school anymore, I still get excited.

With the arrival of June, we see the reappearance of Michigan strawberries. If you have never had a Michigan strawberry, you need to put it on your bucket list. They are, in my opinion, the sweetest and juiciest strawberries ever. Because they are available for only a very short time, from the end of May to about the third week in June, you have to snatch them up while you can and make my Raw Strawberry Jam (page 102) or Strawberry Ice Cream Pie (page 116), or simply freeze them whole to use year-round in smoothies like my Strawberry Hemp Milk Shake (page 70).

June is also a wonderful time to start a garden with small plants from the farmer's market. Tomatoes, lettuce, spinach, beans, peas, peppers, onions, herbs, and, of course, strawberries are all easy to grow and easy to find at your ***local market***. I always try to buy organic plants so I know there are no chemical residues on them. Start with a small and easy-to-manage garden such as a 4 × 6-foot space and work your way up.

JUNE

Here is a sample menu I've put together with a variety of recipes for this month.

breakfast

Pineapple Sweet Bread

•

lunch

Hummus Pizza with Arugula and Wild Mushrooms

•

midday snack

Pineapple Cucumber Gazpacho

•

dinner

Green Chile Enchiladas with Avocado Sauce

•

dessert

Strawberry Ice Cream Pie

Raw Strawberry Jam

As a native Michigander, I have wonderful childhood memories of picking strawberries in June for making jam with my mom and grandma. But I keenly remember the 4 cups of refined sugar that went into each batch, and I cringe at giving my kids all that sugar. Now I make freezer jam using organic berries, no-cook pectin, and almost a third as much sugar for a spread that's about 70 percent raw and 90 percent organic.

Be careful to use the correct measurements for this jam so that you achieve the right consistency. Also, blend the sugar in a food processor until it is very fine so that it dissolves nicely into the fruit. This recipe works with blueberries, raspberries, and peaches as well. I add the juice of one lemon to the batch if using blueberries or peaches.

makes about 5½ cups

1½ cups organic cane sugar

1 (1.6-ounce) packet no-cook freezer jam fruit pectin

4 cups organic strawberries, cored

1. In the bowl of a food processor, process the sugar until it is a fine powder, 45 to 60 seconds. Transfer to a small bowl and add the fruit pectin.
2. In the bowl of a food processor, purée 2 cups of the strawberries until smooth. Pour the purée into the sugar mixture and stir until the sugar is fully dissolved, at least 3 minutes.
3. Pulse the remaining 2 cups strawberries in the food processor until chunky, and pour the strawberries into the bowl of purée. Stir well.
4. Ladle the jam into clean jars, twist on the lids, and let the jam sit at room temperature until set, about 30 minutes. Put the jars in the freezer and freeze overnight. The jam will keep in the freezer for up to a year.

Pineapple Sweet Bread

Do you ever notice that when teenagers walk into your house, they head straight for the kitchen? I can see their eyes scan the counter, looking for something homemade and sweet. When they spy this bread, they make a beeline for it! I love that, because this recipe is gluten and dairy free, but I use organic eggs, so it is not completely vegan. I am okay with that because as a family we don't eat many animal products. Remarkably, this bread takes only about 15 minutes to whip together and you end up with three delicious loaves of bread that you'll be proud to share with family and friends.

makes three 3 × 5½-inch loaves

½ cup grapeseed oil, plus more for pan

1 cup plus 2 tablespoons brown rice flour

1 tablespoon tapioca starch

1¼ teaspoons baking soda

½ teaspoon sea salt

½ teaspoon ground cinnamon

¼ teaspoon ground nutmeg

Pinch ground cloves

1 cup almond meal

2 large eggs

1 large egg white

⅔ cup honey or agave nectar

⅓ cup cashew butter

1 cup coarsely chopped cashews

2 cups finely chopped fresh pineapple

1. Preheat the oven to 300°F. Grease three 3 × 5½-inch loaf pans with grapeseed oil and put them on a baking sheet. Set aside.
2. In a large bowl, whisk together the brown rice flour, tapioca starch, baking soda, salt, cinnamon, nutmeg, and cloves. Whisk in the almond meal. Set aside.
3. In a separate large bowl, combine the eggs, egg white, grapeseed oil, honey, and cashew butter. Add the rice flour mixture and stir just until combined. Add the cashews and pineapple and stir until just incorporated. Divide the batter evenly among the prepared loaf pans.
4. Bake until the loaves are puffed and a wooden skewer inserted into the center comes out clean, 32 to 35 minutes. Let cool for at least 10 minutes before turning out onto wire racks.

Hummus Pizza *with* Arugula *and* Wild Mushrooms

There are so many things you can do with a good pizza crust. I have to admit that there is this amazing little Italian deli a few miles from my house that sells pizza dough, and I sometimes stop in on the way home and buy a bag or two to make for dinner. But it is easy to make your own crust, too. The fun part of pizza making is getting creative with toppings, using whatever we have in the house. We have been putting hummus on our pizza crust for quite some time. On top of the hummus, you can put any greens you have. Sometimes I use watercress or baby spinach for the kids because they are milder, though I love to use fresh spring baby arugula. The sautéed mushrooms add a great texture and pop of flavor.

serves 4

PIZZA DOUGH

- ¾ cup almond milk, homemade (page 34) or store-bought
- 1½ teaspoons grapeseed oil, plus more for bowl
- 1½ teaspoons organic cane sugar
- 1 cup white whole-wheat flour, plus more for kneading
- 1 (¼-ounce) package rapid rise dry yeast
- ½ teaspoon sea salt
- ¾ cup whole-wheat flour

TOPPINGS

- 2 tablespoons grapeseed oil
- 4 cups sliced mixed wild mushrooms
- 1 teaspoon fresh lemon juice
- Sea salt and freshly ground black pepper
- ½ cup hummus, homemade (page 37) or store-bought
- 2 cups loosely packed baby arugula
- ¾ cup sliced cherry tomatoes

1. For the dough, heat the almond milk and oil in a small saucepan set over medium heat until it just begins to simmer. Remove the pan from the heat and set aside.

2. In the bowl of a food processor, pulse the sugar until it is finely ground. Add the white whole-wheat flour, yeast, and salt and pulse two or three times to combine. With the machine running, slowly pour the hot almond milk through the feed tube. Add the whole-wheat flour ¼ cup at a time, pulsing until the dough pulls away from the sides of the bowl.

3. Transfer the dough to a floured work surface. Knead for 4 to 5 minutes, and then shape into a ball. Put the dough in a large oiled bowl and cover loosely with plastic wrap. Let it rise in a warm place until doubled in size, 1 to 1½ hours.

4. Preheat the oven to 425°F. Dust 2 baking sheets lightly with flour and set aside.

5. Punch down the dough and divide it into 4 equal pieces. Lightly dust a cutting board with flour and roll each piece out into a circle that is ⅛ inch thick. Transfer 2 crusts to each of the prepared baking sheets and prick the surfaces all over with a fork. Let rest for 10 minutes.

6. Bake the crusts until golden brown, 12 to 15 minutes. Set aside.

7. For the toppings, heat the oil in a large skillet set over medium-high heat. Add the mushrooms and cook, stirring, until golden, about 4 minutes. Remove the pan from the heat and stir in the lemon juice and season to taste with salt and pepper.

8. Assemble the pizzas by spreading the hummus over the crusts and arranging the arugula, mushrooms, and tomatoes on top. Serve immediately.

Roasted Broccoli *and* Hazelnuts

Against all odds, all of my children love broccoli. In fact, they crave it and will ask for it. My ten-year-old son tells me there are lots of kids in his class who won't eat veggies—even one girl who claims with pride that she has never eaten a green vegetable. This is a problem! Our kids' fast-growing bodies have no other source to draw from other than the food they eat. They'll only grow strong and healthy if they eat well, and that includes vegetables. Start them early and grow their love for good food! I make sure to cut the broccoli thin so that it gets soft for the kids to eat.

serves 4 to 6

1 pound broccoli, cut into strips

1 large shallot, thinly sliced, plus 1 tablespoon minced shallot

3 tablespoons grapeseed oil

Sea salt and freshly ground black pepper

¼ cup coarsely chopped hazelnuts

¼ cup olive oil

1 tablespoon stone ground mustard

1 tablespoon fresh lemon juice

2 teaspoons agave nectar

1. Preheat the oven to 425°F.
2. Put the broccoli and shallots in a medium bowl. Drizzle with the grapeseed oil, season with salt and pepper, and toss well. Spread the broccoli and sliced shallots out on a baking sheet. Roast for 12 minutes. Sprinkle the hazelnuts over the vegetables and roast until the broccoli is just tender, about 7 more minutes.
3. Meanwhile, whisk together olive oil, mustard, lemon juice, agave, and minced shallot in a small bowl until creamy. Drizzle over the broccoli and hazelnuts before serving.

Pineapple Cucumber Gazpacho

Gazpacho is a chilled soup that is typically made with a tomato base, but nowadays this dish can contain endless fruit and vegetable combinations. In my effort to incorporate more raw foods into my diet, I created this recipe, which combines bright, fresh, and extremely healthy ingredients. It's as easy as making a smoothie. I love to serve this soup in martini glasses as an appetizer or first course on the porch in the summer. It is an unexpected gourmet touch to any gathering!

makes 8 cups; serves 4 to 6

½ fresh pineapple, peeled, cored, and chopped

1 English cucumber, peeled and chopped

½ honeydew melon, peeled, seeded, and chopped

½ jalapeño pepper, chopped

½ cup chopped red onion

Sea salt

1 tablespoon chopped fresh mint, for garnish

Working in batches, if necessary, purée the pineapple, cucumber, honeydew, jalapeño, and red onion in a blender until nearly smooth. Season with salt to taste. Chill until ready to serve. Garnish with the mint before serving.

Veggie "Sushi" Roll

Sushi is one of those intimidating dishes that most people won't even try to make at home. It can get a little messy if you're dealing with rice and raw fish, but if you want to make a very easy, impressive, fishless sushi that everyone will love, try this recipe. Once you master this, you may even have the courage to try other more complicated sushi dishes. I think a big part of making sushi is getting to know how to work with the nori, which is a sheet of seaweed. The more you do it, the more confident you will become, and here are a few tips for getting started. Cut the vegetables as thinly as possible—in fact, I often "shred" the jicama and carrot with a vegetable peeler. Also, I go heavy on the avocado, which is a personal preference because I love how it tastes. Nori is very stiff, so be gentle with it and you will be fine. It will slowly absorb the moisture of the vegetables and become softer.

makes 10 pieces

2 nori sheets

1 large avocado, peeled, pitted, and thinly sliced

½ cup bean sprouts

½ cup julienned jicama

½ cup shredded carrot

Sea salt and freshly ground black pepper

¼ teaspoon fresh lemon juice

1. Lay the nori sheets out flat on a work surface.
2. On one end of the nori sheets, lay the avocado in a single row from top to bottom. Layer the sprouts on the avocado, followed by the jicama, and then the carrot. Season with sea salt and freshly ground pepper.
3. Roll the vegetables up in the nori as tightly as possible. Sprinkle lemon juice over the end of the nori sheet and press to seal. Cut each roll into 1-inch pieces. Arrange the sushi on a plate and serve immediately.

Fava Bean and Corn Salad

My favorite room of the house is our covered front porch. Our home is small, but our porch is big, and in the summer we practically live there. Whenever we can, we eat out here too because in Michigan we have to soak up every second of nice weather.

Bean salads are hearty enough to serve as a meal because they provide filling protein in a dish full of fresh ingredients. This salad also works with frozen corn and lima or black beans. Often I throw whatever extra veggies or herbs I have around the house or in the garden into this salad. It's great to whip up a double batch and have the neighbors over for a summer dinner on the porch with Homemade Lemonade (page 115)!

serves 4

2 pounds fresh fava beans, shelled

3 ears of corn, husks and silk removed, cut in half

3 tablespoons olive oil

1 tablespoon rice vinegar

2 teaspoons fresh lime juice

½ teaspoon sea salt

¼ teaspoon freshly ground black pepper

1 red bell pepper, cored, seeded, and chopped

3 scallions, sliced (white and light green parts only)

½ cup thinly sliced red onion

¼ cup chopped fresh cilantro leaves

1. Bring a small saucepan of water to a boil over high heat. Add the beans and cook for 1 minute. Immediately drain in a colander and run under cool water until no longer warm. Remove the skins by squeezing the outer skin between your thumb and fingers and push out the beans.

2. Bring a saucepan of water to a boil over high heat. Add the beans and corn, reduce the heat to medium-low, and simmer until the beans are tender, about 5 minutes. Drain, rinse under cool water, cut the kernels off the cobs, and set aside.

3. In a medium bowl, whisk together the olive oil, vinegar, lime juice, salt, and pepper. Add the red pepper, scallions, red onion, cilantro, and cooked beans and corn, and toss well. Serve immediately or chill.

Quinoa *with* Leeks, Apricots, *and* Toasted Pecans

Whenever I create a new recipe I ask myself a few questions. One is, "What ingredients do I have in my kitchen?" Usually it's whatever is in season. Another is, "How do I make a balanced meal with protein, fiber, antioxidants, and flavor?" This can be tricky, but if you think of nuts and grains for protein, and then grains, fruits, and veggies for fiber and antioxidants, you can begin to piece together something yummy. Lastly I ask myself, "How can I make it fast?" This recipe delivers on all these questions and is versatile because you can switch out different grains, fruits, and nuts using the base recipe. It is packed with vegan protein, fiber, healthy fats, and natural nutrients.

serves 4

2 tablespoons grapeseed oil

1 cup chopped yellow onion

1 cup red or brown quinoa, rinsed and drained

1 teaspoon sea salt, plus more to taste

1 cup pecan, cashew, or almond pieces

½ cup chopped dried apricots, cranberries, or golden raisins

1 tablespoon balsamic vinegar

Freshly ground black pepper

1. Heat the oil in a large skillet set over medium-low heat. Add the onion and cook, stirring, until soft, about 10 minutes. Add 2 cups of water, the quinoa, and salt. Cook until the water is absorbed and the quinoa "tails" have unfurled, about 15 minutes. Remove the pan from the heat.

2. In a small skillet set over low heat, toast the pecans until golden brown, about 4 minutes. Transfer the pecans to the pan of quinoa, add the dried apricots and balsamic vinegar, and season with salt and pepper. Toss well and serve.

tip *homemade lip balm*

At my kids' school in fourth grade, they have a day called "market day" where they have to create an item for sale, price it out, pay wages to workers (aka moms), and sell it to the other students. I've made homemade peppermint lip balm for market day with all three of my kids, and it is always a hit. To me, this is a great way to have fun with your kids and save money at the same time. You can find beeswax at local honey stands or natural food stores. I use peppermint essential oil, but experiment with your favorite aromas.

makes enough to fill two 1-inch tins

1½ teaspoons shredded beeswax

1 tablespoon olive oil

⅛ teaspoon peppermint oil

1. Bring about 1 inch of water to a boil in a saucepan over medium-high heat. Remove the pan from the heat.

2. Put the beeswax and olive oil in a glass measuring cup with a lip for pouring. Put the measuring cup in the pan of hot water and let sit until the beeswax mixture is completely melted. Add the peppermint oil, stir, and pour into two tins. Let cool until solid, about 1 hour.

Green Chile Enchiladas *with* Avocado Sauce

Years ago our family visited a beautiful little town in Mexico called Puerto Escondido. We fell in love with it and have vacationed there for several years. The small town is full of wonderful people and delicious restaurants, as well as lovely homes and hotels.

While there, we walk to the *mercado*, or market, every couple of days for fresh local food. The families in Puerto Escondido inspired this recipe; they prepare the most delicious meals in their restaurants, many of which are run out of their homes and have dirt floors. It is fresh and combines some of my favorite Mexican ingredients. Every family should have a regular "taco night," and you can try this recipe the next time you have yours!

serves 4

Grapeseed oil, for pan

2 medium russet potatoes

3 Anaheim chiles

4 medium tomatillos, husks removed, coarsely chopped

1 cup coarsely chopped yellow onion

2 cups fresh cilantro leaves

2 cups curly parsley leaves

2 garlic cloves

1 cup filtered water

2 teaspoons sea salt

1½ cups unsweetened almond milk, homemade (page 34) or store-bought

¼ teaspoon crushed red pepper flakes

1 (14-ounce) can black beans, rinsed and drained

6 scallions, sliced (white and light green parts only), plus more for garnish

8 corn tortillas

2 large ripe avocados, peeled, pitted, and cut into wedges

5 tablespoons fresh lemon juice

1. Preheat the oven to 400°F. Grease a 9 × 13-inch baking dish with grapeseed oil and set aside.

2. Using a small knife, pierce the potatoes all over and put them on a baking sheet. Bake until the flesh gives when squeezed, about 45 minutes. Let cool until cool enough to handle.

3. Raise the oven temperature to 450°F. Place the chiles directly on the oven rack with a baking sheet positioned on the rack below (to catch any liquid). Roast until the skins blister and begin to blacken, about 10 minutes. Remove the peppers from the oven and wrap them in several layers of damp paper towels. Let stand for 15 minutes. Hold the chiles under cool running water and peel off the skins. Remove the stems and seeds. Reduce the oven temperature to 350°F.

4. In the bowl of a food processor, combine the chiles, tomatillos, onion, cilantro, parsley, garlic, water, and ½ teaspoon of the salt. Purée the mixture until nearly smooth. Transfer to a bowl and set aside.

5. Cut the potatoes in half lengthwise and scoop out the flesh into a medium bowl. Add ¼ cup of the almond milk, the red pepper flakes, and ½ teaspoon of the salt. Mash with a fork until the larger pieces of potato are broken up. Gently stir in the black beans and scallions.

6. Spread a cup of the puréed chile sauce on the bottom of the prepared baking dish.

7. Heat a small skillet over medium heat. Cook the tortillas one at a time until they just begin to turn golden, about 30 seconds. Flip and cook for 30 more seconds. Transfer to a plate.

8. Put ¼ cup of the potato mixture in the centers of each tortilla and roll them up. Put them in the baking dish seam-side down. Pour the remaining chile sauce over the top.

9. Bake until the enchiladas are heated through, about 20 minutes.

10. Meanwhile, in the bowl of a food processor, combine the avocados, remaining almond milk, lemon juice, and remaining 1 teaspoon salt and process until very smooth. The avocado sauce will keep in an airtight container in the refrigerator for 3 days.

11. To serve, put 2 enchiladas on each of 4 serving plates. Top with the avocado sauce and garnish with the sliced scallions.

Roasted Red Peppers *with* Goat Cheese

Not all cheeses are created equal. I am not a fan of dairy, but I do believe that having some dairy in your life is not worrisome. I try to keep dairy down to a few servings a week and that way I don't feel like I am depriving myself. I typically opt for some form of cheese. In the small town of Fennville, just down the road from us, there is a wonderful organic creamery. All of their cheeses come from a herd of the cutest goats you've ever seen, and their goat cheese is my favorite to use in this dish.

I like to crush my rosemary before I use it so it isn't stick-like in my recipes. Put the desired amount into a plastic sandwich bag and crush with a glass cup or rolling pin.

serves 4

2 red bell peppers

1 tablespoon chopped fresh thyme leaves

1 teaspoon crushed fresh rosemary

2 tablespoons chopped fresh chives

2 tablespoons chopped fresh cilantro leaves

1 tablespoon olive oil

4 ounces soft goat cheese (local, if possible)

Sea salt and freshly ground black pepper

1. Preheat the oven to 400°F.
2. Cut the peppers in half and, leaving the stem intact, scoop out the seeds and ribs. Put the peppers cut-side down on a baking sheet.
3. Roast the peppers until they are soft but not burned, about 20 minutes. Transfer the peppers to an airtight container and let cool for 15 minutes.
4. Meanwhile, in a medium bowl, combine the thyme, rosemary, chives, and cilantro. Add the olive oil and cheese, and stir until blended and smooth.
5. To serve, spoon the herbed cheese into the warm pepper halves, and sprinkle each with salt and pepper to taste.

Homemade Lemonade

Lemonade is one of those drinks that we have gotten so used to buying as a mix that we have forgotten how easy it is to make ourselves or even that we can actually make it. When I mentioned to my kids that we should make our own lemonade—after reading the label on a container of the store-bought stuff that said "0 percent juice"—my kids' first response was, "You can do that?" What a perfect example of how dependent we are on the grocery store and how disconnected we are from our food! We went home right away and made our own lemonade with lemons, water, and organic sugar. Then, we made up some variations, adding raspberries, strawberries, and even lavender. Once you make your own, you will never go back to the fake stuff, and your body will thank you!

serves 6

1 cup fresh lemon juice

6 cups cold filtered water

½ cup plus 2 tablespoons organic cane sugar, blended (see page 9)

1 cup strawberries or raspberries, muddled (optional)

3 sprigs lavender, crushed (optional)

1. If you don't like pulp in your lemonade, pour the lemon juice through a fine-mesh strainer. Pour the lemon juice and water into a pitcher. Add the sugar and stir well.
2. For flavored lemonade, stir in the muddled berries or the crushed lavender.
3. Serve in tumblers filled with ice.

Strawberry Ice Cream Pie

This recipe is pretty special because this very pie crust was the beginning of Pure Bars and my company! I still make this pie crust all the time. It is much easier than a pastry crust and massively healthier. It also has more flavor and many more health benefits than a graham cracker crust. I like to soak my almonds overnight to soften them and start the sprouting process, which activates enzymes, making their nutrients more available. I buy dates that have the pits in them and pit them myself, because they're softer and easier to blend.

I make raw pies all summer long with fresh summer fruits layered with spices in this delectable crust. Every year during strawberry season, I make this strawberry pie that tastes like ice cream when frozen!

serves 8 to 10

2 cups almonds

3 cups pitted dates

¼ teaspoon sea salt

3 cups strawberries, hulled

1 cup cashews

1. Put the almonds in a large bowl and fill the bowl with water to cover by 1 inch. Let soak for 8 hours.
2. Drain the almonds and put them in the bowl of a food processor. Add 2 cups of the dates and the salt and process until the ingredients are finely chopped and begin to stick together. Press the mixture into a 9-inch pie dish and freeze for 30 minutes.
3. In a food processor, combine 2 cups of the strawberries, the remaining 1 cup dates, and the cashews and process until smooth and creamy. Pour the mixture into the pie crust and top with the remaining 1 cup strawberries.
4. Freeze until firm, 2 hours. The pie will keep in the freezer for up to 3 days.

tip edible flowers

Midsummer is a perfect time to add flowers to your salads, appetizers, and main dishes—not just as a garnish but also as a part of the actual dish. There are many beautiful varieties of edible flowers, which can turn a mundane dish into a gourmet masterpiece. Many edible flowers have been used throughout the centuries for their medicinal benefits. Some of my favorites that are very easy to grow in your garden or in pots are below.

- Calendula, also known as "poor man's saffron," can be used just like saffron. Sprinkle the petals into rice and vegetable dishes. It is very high in antioxidants and known for its anti-inflammatory properties.
- Chamomile petals are wonderful for making tea but also great to add to salads, breakfast porridge, and soups. It's known to soothe digestion, relax muscles, and calm the senses.
- Pansies and violets are beautiful and completely edible. Place the entire flowers and leaves in salads and on crackers with a spread to create a stunning dish. They are also high in antioxidants and a strong anti-inflammatory.
- Nasturtiums are another annual that have a great flavor and are often used whole in salads. You can also chop the petals and add to softened butter or cheese as a spread or use in pasta dishes. Known as a detoxifier, they help clear your sinuses when you have a cold.

july

Grandma's Blueberry Buckle

Warm Blueberry Buckwheat with Hazelnuts

Cherry, Cucumber, and Almond Salad

Sweet Corn Pudding

Pistachio Couscous with Orange Zest

Marinated Haricots Verts and Cherry Pasta Salad

Grilled Garlic and Summer Squash Skewers with Chimichurri

The Perfect Veggie Burger

Watermelon Mint Salad

Blueberry Mojito

Cherry Chocolate Mousse

Vacation, camping, fireworks, boat rides, cookouts, garden vegetables, farmer's markets, and bike rides . . . these are the things that pop into my head when I think about July. There is a ***joyful urgency to savor every day*** of this time of year.

I have wonderful memories of camping up north at the rustic D. H. Day Campground near Sleeping Bear Dunes National Lakeshore with my family each summer. I'm talking "outhouse only" type camping, by the way. My dad would look for the largest, most remote campsite in the wooded rustic campground on the shores of Lake Michigan. We would borrow my grandparents' pop-up trailer and explore the lake and dunes for a week.

July is the month to ***make memories***, and so often great food is a part of those memories. Think of the tastes and smells that you associate with summer. Most likely they are from foods that are harvested this time of year. In the summer I strive to eat mainly local foods, and I love the ***variety of fresh produce available*** this time of year. The garden and farmer's markets provide virtually all we need to live on. My body soaks up the wonderful sunshine and fresh, just-picked produce that this month offers.

JULY

Here is a sample menu I've put together with a variety of recipes for this month.

breakfast

Grandma's Blueberry Buckle

•

lunch

Marinated Haricots Verts and Cherry Pasta Salad

•

midday snack

Watermelon Mint Salad

•

dinner

The Perfect Veggie Burger

•

dessert

Cherry Chocolate Mousse

Grandma's Blueberry Buckle

One of the best parts about going to Grandma's house was discovering the delicious things that came from her kitchen. I especially looked forward to her freshly baked breakfast goodies, like this fantastic buckle.

A buckle is sort of like a coffee cake, so you can bet on it being sweet and indulgent. I am a firm believer that homemade baked goods made with rich ingredients are much better for us than any processed food, and they can be enjoyed in moderation. I've tweaked it a bit, making it healthier without sacrificing the flavor and texture. Rice flour makes it gluten free, and substituting almond milk for dairy gives it a touch more flavor.

makes one 9 × 13-inch cake

TOPPING

½ cup packed organic brown sugar

½ cup brown rice flour

½ teaspoon ground cinnamon

1 cup chopped walnuts

½ cup coconut oil, at room temperature

BUCKLE

Grapeseed oil, for pan

1½ cups brown rice flour

1½ cups white rice flour

1 tablespoon tapioca starch

2 teaspoons baking powder

½ teaspoon sea salt

1 cup almond meal

½ cup coconut oil, at room temperature

1 cup organic cane sugar

3 large eggs

1½ teaspoons vanilla extract

1½ cups almond milk, homemade (page 34) or store-bought

2 cups fresh blueberries

1. For the topping, in a medium bowl, combine the brown sugar, rice flour, and cinnamon. Add the walnuts and coconut oil and stir just to incorporate. The mixture will be clumpy. Set aside.
2. Preheat the oven to 325°F. Grease a 9 × 13-inch baking pan with grapeseed oil and set aside.
3. For the buckle, sift together the brown and white rice flours, tapioca starch, baking powder, and salt in a medium bowl. Stir in the almond meal.

4. In the bowl of a stand mixer fitted with the paddle attachment, beat the coconut oil and sugar on high speed until combined, about 2 minutes. Beat in the eggs one at a time, and then beat in the vanilla. Add 1 cup of the dry ingredients and ¼ cup of the almond milk, and beat to combine. Repeat until all the dry ingredients and almond milk have been incorporated, and then beat for 1 more minute. Fold in 1 cup of the blueberries.

5. Pour the batter into the prepared baking pan. Sprinkle the remaining 1 cup blueberries over the top and scatter the topping over the blueberries.

6. Bake until a wooden skewer inserted into the center comes out clean, about 45 minutes. Let cool on a wire rack for at least 10 minutes before serving. Serve warm.

Warm Blueberry Buckwheat *with* Hazelnuts

Buckwheat for breakfast? Yes, please! Hazelnuts are a divine complement to warm buckwheat, fresh blueberries in season, and almond milk. This simple breakfast is packed with nutritious grains, fruits, and spices, yet tastes like dessert. And because it cooks up so fast, it's also a great camping breakfast.

serves 4 to 6

1 cup whole-grain buckwheat cereal

¼ teaspoon sea salt

⅛ teaspoon grated nutmeg

⅓ cup honey

⅓ cup fresh blueberries

¼ cup chopped hazelnuts

½ cup almond milk, homemade (page 34) or store-bought

1. Put 3 cups of water in a medium saucepan and bring to a boil over high heat. Stir in the buckwheat, salt, and nutmeg. Cover the pan, reduce the heat to low, and simmer until the liquid is absorbed and the buckwheat is soft, about 10 minutes. Drain any excess water from the cooked buckwheat

2. Spoon the buckwheat into serving bowls. Stir in the honey, blueberries, and hazelnuts. Serve hot with the almond milk poured over the top.

Cherry, Cucumber, *and* Almond Salad

This time of year cherries are everywhere in Michigan. In Traverse City, we celebrate the National Cherry Festival, where air shows, music concerts, wine tasting, and tons of amazing cherries and cherry foods are everywhere! At our local orchards, cherries are ready for the picking in July. This salad beautifully features summer's delicious fresh cherries, which add a burst of flavor to everything, especially the dark sweet Michigan cherries that I like to use. I also love how beautiful, fresh, and crunchy this salad is with the jicama and cucumber.

serves 6 to 8

¼ cup olive oil

1 tablespoon white balsamic vinegar

1 teaspoon Dijon mustard

½ teaspoon sea salt

¼ teaspoon freshly ground black pepper

1½ pounds cherries, cut in half and pitted

1 hothouse cucumber, chopped

1 medium jicama, peeled and chopped (about 2 cups)

½ cup sliced almonds

In a large bowl, whisk together the oil, vinegar, mustard, salt, and pepper. Add the cherries, cucumber, jicama, and almonds, and toss well. Serve at room temperature or chilled.

tip *green lawn care*

My kids and pets love to play in the grass. They roll around, slide, and lie in our yard during the summer months. It didn't take me long to decide I will never spray fertilizers or unnatural chemicals on my lawn again. Interestingly, in 2009 Ontario, Canada, banned the use of cosmetic pesticides on lawns, gardens, school yards, and parks, citing strong evidence from medical experts like the Canadian Cancer Society that reducing exposure to pesticides was important. Not only do researchers from Canada and the United States agree that there is a link between pesticide exposure and certain cancers, but also when fertilizers and herbicides are sprayed onto our grass, some of these chemicals are carried off by the rain and flow into our local streams and lakes.

To me the solution is simple and obvious. If we don't spray chemicals on our grass, we save money and protect our earth and ourselves from harmful chemicals. I have pulled quite a few weeds in my lifetime, but I also don't let weeds bother me because they are usually native plants and have beauty. Below are some ways to have a happy and healthy lawn without harmful chemicals!

- Let your grass grow and stay longer. It'll mean less mowing and less need to water.
- Water your lawn infrequently. This makes the grass roots grow deeper, strengthening your lawn, and makes it more difficult for weeds to grow.
- Use vinegar to control weeds in driveway cracks and sidewalks. Pour white vinegar directly onto the weeds, or make a solution of one part vinegar to one part water to spray on pesky weeds. Use on a sunny, dry day.
- Use a mulching mower that puts clippings back on the lawn. It will naturally fertilize and protect your lawn.
- If you feel like you must fertilize or control weeds, look for all-natural and low-phosphorous products like Organics Rx.

Sweet Corn Pudding

Corn is often overlooked, as green and orange veggies get most of our attention. But corn is full of incredible nutrients. High in folate, which protects against birth defects, heart disease, and colon cancer, corn is also a great source of the B vitamin thiamine, which promotes healthy brain and memory function. It has antioxidants and carotenoids that have been found to help decrease the chance of lung cancer and colon cancer. It is also a good source of dietary fiber and vitamin C. So there's no reason to feel bad about enjoying this delightful summer vegetable!

However, as I mentioned earlier, it is important to know that corn is one of the most genetically modified foods, so buying organic is crucial. Also, eating fresh, whole corn is very different from eating corn products, which are often highly processed. So go fresh!

serves 4

4 ears of corn, husks and silk removed

2 teaspoons grapeseed oil or coconut oil

½ cup filtered water

¾ cup plain coconut milk yogurt or other nondairy yogurt

3 tablespoons honey

⅛ teaspoon grated nutmeg

¼ teaspoon ground cinnamon

⅛ teaspoon sea salt

2 medium peaches, pitted and chopped

1. Cut the corn kernels off the cobs and put the kernels in a medium saucepan. Using a metal spoon, scrape any pulp left on the cobs into the saucepan. Add the oil and cook over medium-low heat for 4 minutes.
2. Add the water, raise the heat to medium-high, and bring to a boil. Reduce the heat to low, cover, and simmer until the kernels are soft, about 17 minutes.
3. Add the yogurt, honey, nutmeg, cinnamon, and salt. Simmer, stirring frequently, until the mixture thickens, about 10 minutes. Stir in the peaches and cook for 2 more minutes. Serve hot.

Pistachio Couscous *with* Orange Zest

Pistachios are the potato chip of the nut world. Once you start eating them, it's really hard to stop. The good news is that they are exponentially better for you than chips and are especially good for your heart, as research has shown that they can help lower bad cholesterol. They are also high in important antioxidants. There is nothing like sitting outside on a warm summer day, cracking pistachios and drinking a cold beer. I have been a huge fan of this nut ever since my mom would serve neon-green pistachio pudding and pistachio ice cream when I was a kid. I now eat them in their non-neon form. This easy summer recipe pairs the richness of this delightful nut with a juicy orange. It's perfectly balanced and great for a hot summer night (and cold beer).

serves 4 to 5

1½ cups filtered water

¼ teaspoon sea salt

1½ cups couscous

2 tablespoons olive oil

Zest and juice from 1 medium orange

¾ cup roasted shelled pistachios, coarsely chopped

¼ cup chopped fresh flat-leaf parsley

1. Bring the water and ⅛ teaspoon of the salt to a boil in a medium saucepan set over high heat. Stir in the couscous, remove the pan from the heat, cover, and let stand for 5 minutes.
2. Meanwhile, in a medium bowl, whisk together the olive oil, orange juice and zest, and remaining ⅛ teaspoon salt. Add the couscous, pistachios, and parsley, and stir well. Serve warm, at room temperature, or chilled.

CRANBERRY LEEK QUINOA page 181

PICKLED VEGETABLES page 53

VEGAN TACOS page 40 *(opposite page)*

EGG NOODLES WITH WILD MUSHROOMS AND SPRING GREENS page 73

ASPARAGUS WITH TURMERIC-SPICED ALMONDS page 75 *(opposite page)*

EGGPLANT LOVE LASAGNE page 168

WINTER GARLIC AND VEGETABLE STEW page 21 *(opposite page)*

PEPPERMINT BROWNIES page 218 *(above left)*
AND RAW CHOCOLATE CHIP COOKIES page 43

RHUBARB BREAKFAST CRISP page 86 *(above right)*

WARM BLUEBERRY BUCKWHEAT WITH HAZELNUTS page 124 *(opposite page)*

BIBB LETTUCE WITH GRAPEFRUIT, AVOCADO, AND CREAMY AVOCADO DRESSING page 54

WALNUT-STUFFED SQUASH page 215 *(opposite page)*

WATERCRESS, CUCUMBER, AND TOASTED PECAN SALAD page 90 *(above left)*

THE PERFECT VEGGIE BURGER page 132 *(above right)*

GRILLED GARLIC AND SUMMER SQUASH SKEWERS WITH CHIMICHURRI page 130 *(opposite page)*

MARINATED HARICOTS VERTS AND CHERRY PASTA SALAD page 129

ROASTED ROOT VEGETABLES WITH HONEY SAUCE page 20 *(opposite page)*

HUMMUS PIZZA WITH ARUGULA AND WILD MUSHROOMS page 104

Marinated Haricots Verts *and* Cherry Pasta Salad

One of my favorite Pure Bars (and also a best seller) is our Cherry Cashew. It was the second flavor I created in my kitchen after the Chocolate Brownie one. I used unsweetened organic tart cherries because of the amazing health benefits and flavor pop, and paired them with the rich taste of cashews. This recipe plays off the successful combination of cherry and cashews and creates a satisfying and simple lunch or dinner. Haricots verts are a French variety of green beans that are longer and thinner than what we typically see in the United States. If you can't find them, just use small, thin green beans instead.

serves 4

2 cups (about 8 ounces) trimmed haricots verts or small green beans, cut into 2-inch pieces

¼ cup olive oil

Zest and juice of 2 medium lemons

Sea salt and freshly ground black pepper

1 cup dried cherries

1 (12-ounce) package small whole wheat pasta

¾ cup roasted unsalted cashews

1 medium red onion, thinly sliced

1. Bring a medium saucepan of water to a boil over high heat. Add the haricots verts and cook just until they turn bright green, 1 to 2 minutes. Drain and run them under cool running water to stop the cooking process. Set aside.
2. In a large bowl, whisk together the olive oil and lemon juice, and season with salt and pepper to taste. Add the haricots verts and cherries, and toss well. Let stand for 15 minutes.
3. Meanwhile, bring a large pot of salted water to a boil over high heat. Add the pasta and cook according to the package directions for al dente. Drain into a colander and let cool to room temperature.
4. Add the pasta, cashews, red onion, and lemon zest to the haricots verts mixture, and toss gently to combine. Season with salt and pepper to taste. Serve at room temperature or chilled.

Grilled Garlic *and* Summer Squash Skewers *with* Chimichurri

Summer begs for grilling. Many people think a grill is just for meat, but once you've had a little experience with grilling fresh produce, the grill will become your best friend in the hot summer months. There is something unique about cooking on a grill—it just makes the flavors of ingredients blend superbly well and brings out the best in vegetables.

In this recipe I combine a sauce called chimichurri—a green, herby sauce usually used to marinate meat—with a colorful array of vegetables. The hearty squash really takes on the chimichurri flavors. It's the perfect summer grilling dish!

makes six 10-inch skewers

CHIMICHURRI

¼ cup finely chopped fresh parsley leaves

¼ cup finely chopped fresh basil leaves

3 garlic cloves, minced

½ cup extra-virgin olive oil

1 teaspoon sea salt

½ teaspoon freshly ground black pepper

SKEWERS

12 large garlic cloves

Olive oil, for drizzling

1 medium zucchini, sliced ½ inch thick

1 medium yellow squash, sliced ½ inch thick

1 red bell pepper, cored, seeded, and cut into 1-inch pieces

1. For the chimichurri, in a large bowl, combine the parsley, basil, garlic, olive oil, salt, and pepper. Set aside.
2. Preheat the oven to 350°F.
3. For the skewers, place the garlic cloves on a small baking sheet, drizzle with the olive oil, and toss well. Roast until lightly golden, about 10 minutes. Transfer to the bowl of sauce. Add the zucchini, yellow squash, and bell pepper to the bowl and toss well. Thread the vegetables and garlic cloves onto skewers and set aside.
4. Preheat a grill pan over high heat or an outdoor grill to high. Grill the skewers until lightly brown and cooked through, about 3 minutes per side. Drizzle with any remaining sauce and serve hot.

tip *organic wine*

It seems that "wine o'clock" happens more often and earlier in the summer. With the great weather and long summer days, opening a good bottle of wine just seems natural.

I've always been a fan of organic wines because of their purity and authentic flavor, and they don't have any pesticides or herbicides to tarnish the taste or your health. Many organic wines also do not contain sulfites, which can lead to headaches. Recently I've become intrigued with biodynamic wine.

The biodynamic method of growing grapes focuses on sustainability and all the parts of the environment that work together—from insects and soil to the earth's rotation, phases of the moon, and angle of the sun—to grow grapes with amazing and completely natural flavor. There is a spiritual aspect as well that is pulled from ancient methods of farming that teach the best ways to prune and handle plants. All biodynamic wines are also naturally organic and most do not include sulfites.

I feel that biodynamic wines are always richer in flavor and have much more personality than other wines. And one of the best benefits of drinking these completely natural wines is that you don't end up with a headache the next day. But don't take my word for it—do your own wine-tasting experiments!

The Perfect Veggie Burger

What's perfect for one person may not be for another, but trust me when I say you will think this veggie burger as near to perfect as one can get. It's hearty, mild in flavor, and rich—a fantastic mimic of a beef burger. I don't care for spicy veggie burgers or overly flavorful ones, because I think the most important characteristic is a moist, meaty texture, which the mushrooms and grapeseed oil help achieve. I sometimes like to make my own bread crumbs using a local organic sourdough bread. I just let it sit on the counter to dry out a bit, and then pulse it into fine crumbs.

These burgers are great served with the usual bun, lettuce, tomato, red onion, and condiments. I have also baked this in a bread pan for a homemade meat loaf, and served it with Garlic and Thyme Mashed Potatoes (page 78).

serves 4 to 6

1 cup chopped yellow onion

½ cup chopped celery

¼ cup grapeseed oil

1 teaspoon sea salt

½ teaspoon freshly ground black pepper

6 slices sprouted wheat bread or gluten-free bread, toasted

8 ounces cremini or baby bella mushrooms

½ cup loosely packed fresh flat-leaf parsley

1½ teaspoons tapioca starch

1 tablespoon tamari

1. In the bowl of a food processor, combine the onion and celery and pulse until finely chopped.
2. Heat 2 tablespoons of the oil in a nonstick skillet set over medium heat. Add the onion mixture, salt, and pepper and cook, stirring, until golden brown, about 7 minutes. Transfer to a medium bowl and set aside.
3. Tear the bread into 2-inch pieces, put them in the food processor, and pulse until most of the mixture is in fine crumbs. Transfer to the bowl of onion mixture.
4. Put the mushrooms and parsley in the food processor (no need to wipe it out) and pulse until finely chopped. Add the mushroom mixture to the onion mixture.
5. In a small bowl, combine the tapioca starch and tamari. Sprinkle it over the onion mixture. Using your hands, work the onion mixture until it begins to stick together and is almost pasty. Let stand for 10 minutes before forming into 4 patties about 4 inches across.
6. Heat the remaining 2 tablespoons oil in a large nonstick skillet set over medium-low heat. Cook the patties until golden brown, about 4 minutes. Flip the patties and cook until the second side is golden brown, 3 to 4 minutes. Serve hot.

tip *cooking with tapioca*

Tapioca is one of those ingredients that was once used frequently (I see it in my grandmother's old recipes) but definitely fell off the radar for a while. Lately, though, it has been becoming more popular because it is gluten free. Tapioca can be used as a thickener and binder and is most often used for sauces and pies and other desserts. Remember tapioca pudding that we called "fish eye pudding"? Well, today's tapioca takes on many different forms.

Tapioca comes from the root of the cassava plant, which grows in tropical climates. I use the starch or flour form wherever I would use flour or cornstarch. I like tapioca because it is easier to work with than cornstarch; it thickens very quickly when heated and the resulting dish freezes well, too (sauces with cornstarch can become mealy). Tapioca also has a very mild flavor, so it blends easily with other ingredients. Because it is simply made of ground-up cassava root, it is a more whole and less processed food than flour and cornstarch, and that is always a big plus!

Watermelon Mint Salad

Do you know that watermelon is highly nutritious? Like tomatoes, it is packed with lycopene, an important phytonutrient that has been linked to improved cardio-vascular health. I love tomatoes, but nothing beats a sweet, juicy watermelon. It also contains significant amounts of other important nutrients, including beta-carotene and vitamin C. It's very easy to cut up a watermelon and serve it just as is, and there is certainly nothing wrong with that! But if you want to add even more flavor and health, try this salad. I have the kids run out to the garden to collect the fresh mint. It is truly a local, seasonal dish. It also makes a terrific salad for a Friday night barbecue at your friend's house when you don't have time to cook, and actually has a surprising "kick" that all the macho guys will love!

serves 4 to 6

1 (5-pound) seedless watermelon

¼ cup finely chopped mint leaves

1 tablespoon fresh lime juice

½ teaspoon sea salt

¼ teaspoon cayenne pepper

1. Cut the watermelon flesh into bite-size pieces, or use a melon baller to make rounds, and discard the rind. Put the melon in a large bowl, sprinkle with the mint, lime juice, salt, and cayenne, and toss gently.
2. Chill for at least 1 hour before serving cold.

Blueberry Mojito

Warning: This drink goes down fast, so be careful! I am a firm believer in the benefits of treating your cocktails like your food, making them with only fresh, organic ingredients. Many of us throw health out the window when we're drinking alcohol, because we just figure we've already ruined the day's diet so why worry about it. However, drinking healthy cocktails rather than libations with highly processed ingredients is not only better for your body, but it also lessens the effects of overindulging, if you know what I mean.

serves 1

⅓ cup fresh blueberries

8 mint leaves, chopped

2 tablespoons agave nectar or honey

2 tablespoons fresh lime juice

½ cup sparkling water

1 (1.5-ounce) shot of rum

In a tumbler, muddle together the blueberries, mint, and agave until thoroughly crushed. Add the lime juice, sparkling water, and rum. Top with ice, stir, and serve.

Cherry Chocolate Mousse

This recipe is to die for, especially when made with fresh, seasonal sweet cherries. Combined with nondairy ingredients, this mousse is way too healthy to taste this good. If your kids ask for candy, give them this. If your significant other asks for ice cream, make this. If you are having a major chocolate craving, reach for this! If you have to bring a dish to a potluck, you will be revered within your social circle for the complexity of this mousse, yet little will they know how easy it is. You can thank me after you've eaten it!

serves 6

1½ cups semisweet vegan chocolate chips

½ cup agave nectar

1½ teaspoons vanilla extract

1 (14-ounce) package firm tofu

1½ cups cherries, pitted, or 1 cup frozen cherries, thawed and patted dry

1. Melt the chocolate chips in a double boiler or in a small pan set inside a medium pan that has 2 inches of boiling water in it. Add the agave and vanilla, and stir well. Remove the pan from the heat.
2. In the bowl of a food processor, pulse the tofu until smooth. Add the chocolate mixture and blend until completely smooth. Add the cherries and pulse one or two times to incorporate.
3. Spoon the mixture into six 6-ounce ramekins. Cover and chill for at least 20 minutes or up to 3 days.

tip *cooking with tofu*

I have a love/hate relationship with tofu. On the one hand, it can be highly processed and made with genetically altered soy, which is a big no-no. On the other hand, it is high in protein, calcium, iron, and magnesium, which are all great nutrients for vegetarians. And, because it's fermented, it has probiotics, which are beneficial for our bodies.

I have to admit to being fearful of tofu's taste and texture, so I mainly use it as a thickener in dishes where it is essentially invisible, but occasionally I will use it in recipes like my Red Chard with Sweet Peppers and Tofu (page 152), in which the tofu wonderfully absorbs the flavors of the dish.

Look for tofu that is certified organic and non-GMO, as well as locally made, if possible. I have been lucky to find a local source, but I also know of people who make their own tofu. From what I understand, it is easy to make but time-consuming. Try a few tofu recipes with your family and see whether you can work this wonderfully nutritious food into your diet.

august

Peaches and Cream Amaranth Porridge

Egg and Spinach Phyllo

Fennel Mushroom Pupusas with Spicy Pineapple Dipping Sauce

Heirloom Tomato and Summer Fruit Salad with Creamy Vinaigrette

Walnut Pâté

Eggplant Bruschetta

Lemon Dill Potato Salad

Red Chard with Sweet Peppers and Tofu

Coconut Boysenberry Smoothie

Frozen Sugared Limes

Peach Raspberry Crostata

How is it that summer seemed to last forever when you were a kid but now that you're all grown up it just flies by? When I was a kid, August days seemed endless. Every day was a different adventure. Lake Michigan was warm enough to swim in without getting numb, and we would spend long days making sand castles and jumping in the waves.

Trips to Grandma and Grandpa's house and various cousins' houses resulted in one ***backyard barbecue*** after another. The aunts all bustled around the kitchen making potato salad and cutting up veggies and sweet pickles while Grandpa manned the grill.

August eating means snacking on juicy blackberries and plump peaches, and sipping homemade sun tea—everything fresh and ripe! The ***gardens are filled with heirloom tomatoes and fresh herbs*** that we can use to make Heirloom Tomato and Summer Fruit Salad (page 146). There's plenty of fresh dill for Lemon Dill Potato Salad (page 150) and deep purple eggplant for Eggplant Bruschetta (page 149). Life is plentiful and rich during August!

AUGUST

Here is a sample menu I've put together with
a variety of recipes for this month.

breakfast

Peaches and Cream Amaranth Porridge

•

lunch

Lemon Dill Potato Salad and Walnut Pâté

•

midday snack

Frozen Sugared Limes

•

dinner

Red Chard with Sweet Peppers and Tofu

•

dessert

Peach Raspberry Crostata

Peaches *and* Cream Amaranth Porridge

Roasting probably isn't the first thing you think of doing with fruit, but it really brings out the flavor. Seasonal summer and fall fruits like peaches, plums, and pears take especially well to this preparation, and they pair deliciously with hearty grains.

I get many questions from people about how vegetarians and vegans get their protein. It may sound surprising, but you can get all the protein you need from plant sources. Cooked amaranth reminds me of the cream of wheat my mom used to make us growing up, and it blends well with sweet fruit, cinnamon, honey, and creamy almond milk. The bonus with a breakfast like this is that you get complete protein from the grains as well as fiber, natural carbs, and antioxidants that will keep you and your family healthy and strong all day.

serves 4

2 ripe peaches

1 tablespoon fresh lemon juice

1 tablespoon organic cane sugar

1 cup amaranth

2 tablespoons coconut oil

⅛ teaspoon sea salt

½ teaspoon ground cinnamon

2 to 4 tablespoons honey or maple syrup

1 cup almond milk, homemade (page 34) or store-bought

1. Preheat the oven to 400°F.
2. Halve the peaches and remove the pits. Put the peaches cut-side up in a shallow baking dish with ¼ inch of water in the bottom. Sprinkle the peach halves with the lemon juice and sugar.
3. Roast until the peaches are soft and have started to brown, about 35 minutes. Set aside to cool.
4. Meanwhile, in a medium saucepan set over medium heat, combine 3 cups of water, the amaranth, coconut oil, and salt. Bring to a boil and simmer until the water is absorbed and the grains are tender, about 20 minutes.
5. Divide the amaranth among 4 bowls. Slice the roasted peaches and place on top of the amaranth. Sprinkle with the cinnamon, drizzle with ½ to 1 tablespoon of the honey, and pour ¼ cup of the almond milk over the top of each serving. Serve immediately.

Egg *and* Spinach Phyllo

This is my favorite breakfast for when I have people to impress. If I am having family or friends over for brunch, I will make this—in under an hour—and revel in the compliments. Each ramekin is a perfect little individual gourmet breakfast or lunch that pairs wonderfully with fruit or a salad. If you don't have individual ramekins, simply make these in a greased large muffin tin. You can easily pop the individual servings out of the tin and onto a plate.

I have found that you can buy organic phyllo dough that even comes in whole-wheat or spelt varieties at your local natural food store.

serves 4

¼ cup grapeseed oil, plus more for ramekins

5 large eggs, beaten

1½ cups coarsely chopped spinach

½ cup crumbled feta cheese

1 tablespoon chopped scallion (white and light green parts only)

⅛ teaspoon sea salt

⅛ teaspoon freshly ground black pepper

8 sheets frozen phyllo dough, thawed

1. Preheat the oven to 350°F. Grease four 4-ounce ramekins with grapeseed oil.
2. In a medium bowl, combine the eggs, spinach, feta, scallion, salt, and pepper. Set aside.
3. Unroll the phyllo dough and immediately cover it with plastic wrap to prevent the sheets from drying out and cracking. Remove one sheet of phyllo dough and put it on a clean work surface (don't worry if the phyllo breaks; it will still work fine). Brush the sheet lightly with the oil, coating the entire surface. Put another sheet of phyllo on top and brush with oil. Repeat 2 more times. Cutting along the shorter edge, cut the stack into 4 pieces. Put 2 pieces in an "X" shape over a prepared ramekin and gently press the dough into the bottom. Fill with ½ cup of the egg mixture. Bring the ends of the phyllo together above the filling and pinch to seal. Repeat with the remaining 2 phyllo pieces for the second ramekin.
4. Repeat step 3 for the remaining 2 ramekins. Put the filled ramekins on a baking sheet.
5. Bake until golden brown on top, about 20 minutes. Set aside for at least 5 minutes before serving hot or at room temperature.

Fennel Mushroom Pupusas *with* Spicy Pineapple Dipping Sauce

A popular dish in El Salvador, pupusas are corn-based tortillas typically filled with meat, cheese, and spices. I make mine with fruit, veggies, and mushrooms, along with a fantastic Sriracha sauce, and serve it as an appetizer or a main dish.

Fennel is a glorious vegetable! If you haven't grown it or cooked with it, you need to give it a shot. It has a delightful mild licorice flavor, and while it is best known for its bulb, all parts of the plant are edible. My neighbor has a huge fennel plant growing in her yard this time of year and when we walk by we always pick the feathery tips off to chew on. Luckily, she doesn't mind! Fennel and fennel fronds are also great to add to salads and vegetables.

serves 4

1½ cups coarsely chopped pineapple

1 tablespoon Sriracha chili sauce

2 ounces button mushrooms

2 tablespoons chopped fresh flat-leaf parsley

1 teaspoon chopped fresh oregano

3 tablespoons plus 2 teaspoons grapeseed oil

1 leek, washed well and finely chopped

⅓ cup finely chopped fennel bulb

¾ teaspoon sea salt

½ cup bread crumbs

2 cups organic corn flour

1½ cups filtered water

1 cup shredded green cabbage

1. In the bowl of a food processor, combine 1¼ cups of the pineapple and the Sriracha. Blend until nearly smooth. Transfer to a small bowl and set aside. Finely chop the remaining ¼ cup pineapple and set aside.

2. In the bowl of a food processor, pulse the mushrooms, parsley, and oregano until finely chopped. Transfer to a separate medium bowl.

3. Heat 2 teaspoons of the grapeseed oil in a medium skillet set over medium heat. Add the leek, fennel, and ¼ teaspoon of the salt. Cook, stirring often, until softened, about 3 minutes. Transfer to the bowl with the mushrooms. Add the bread crumbs and stir well.

4. In a medium bowl, combine the corn flour, remaining ½ teaspoon salt, and water and knead until it forms a moist (but not sticky) dough. Divide into 16 pieces and form each into a ball. Press the dough into disks that are about ⅛ inch thick. Put a scant tablespoon of the filling on one half of each disk. Fold the dough over and pinch and smooth the edges to seal.

5. Heat the remaining 3 tablespoons oil in a large skillet set over medium heat. Cook the pupusas until golden, 2 to 3 minutes. Flip the pupusas and cook until golden on the second side, about 2 more minutes.

6. To serve, divide the cabbage among 4 serving plates and put 4 pupusas on each plate. Garnish with the sauce and reserved chopped pineapple and serve hot.

Heirloom Tomato *and* Summer Fruit Salad *with* Creamy Vinaigrette

Remember the age-old question: Is tomato a fruit or a vegetable? Technically, it is a fruit and that is exactly how I use it in this salad. I am a huge believer in homegrown, heirloom, farmer's market fresh tomatoes. There is a massive difference in flavor between a fresh-off-the-vine heirloom tomato and a store-bought, greenhouse-grown variety that has ripened in a warehouse.

Heirloom tomatoes are sweeter and all around more flavorful, and to me there is no comparison! In this salad they blend perfectly with the other fruits, and I daresay that even children who shy away from tomatoes will gobble them up. We eat lots of tomatoes in my house because they are delicious and packed with lycopene and antioxidants shown to help prevent cancer and protect skin from harmful UV rays—important for fair-skinned people like me!

serves 6

2 cups red grapes

2 mangos, peeled, pitted, and chopped

2 kiwi, peeled and cut into wedges

3 heirloom tomatoes, cored and chopped

2 tablespoons grapeseed oil

2½ teaspoons cider vinegar

1 tablespoon chopped fresh mint

½ teaspoon sea salt

1. In a medium bowl, combine the grapes, mango, kiwi, and all but ½ cup of the tomato. Toss gently.
2. In the bowl of a food processor or blender, combine the remaining ½ cup tomato, oil, vinegar, mint, and salt. Blend until smooth and creamy.
3. Drizzle the vinaigrette over the fruit, or pour it into a bowl on the side for dipping, and serve.

tip *vinegar*

Vinegar is an interesting product that has been around for centuries. Most likely, it was discovered by accident when wine and other fermented drinks "soured." Fermenting alcohol, essentially the next step after wine, produces vinegar. So, grapes are fermented into wine, which can then be fermented into vinegar. There are many different types of vinegar, differing mainly in flavor and strength. You can make vinegar from fruits, grains, vegetables, and seeds, or just about anything that you can think of. The most popular kinds are distilled, rice, apple cider, and balsamic.

The vinegar used in most salad dressings actually helps your body utilize the calcium in the leafy greens. It also blocks some of the absorption of the fats from the oils that are also often used in dressings. Pretty cool, huh? It has also been shown to stabilize blood sugar levels, curb your appetite, lower cholesterol, and help protect from certain cancers. I don't know about you, but to me, those are mighty good reasons to keep a bottle on hand. And of course, there are the antimicrobial cleaning benefits that I talk about on page 77.

Walnut Pâté

Sometimes when I really like the way something tastes, I wonder if other people will like it too, especially because I have changed my diet to eat much more whole, real food and much less processed food. Every now and then there are things I have come to like that others don't. So whenever I absolutely love a dish, I need to try it out on others. A "walnut pâté" sounds kind of weird, but it's fabulous.

Created by Andrea Lambert, this recipe was a winner in one of our Pure Vegetarian Recipe contests. I brought it to a party once, and everyone absolutely raved about it—but the funny thing is that no one could tell what was in it. You can whip up this recipe in no time flat. And because it is made with raw, whole foods, it provides amazing nutrients: omega-3s and protein from the walnuts, antioxidants in the pepper, and added fiber in the celery and scallion.

makes about 2 cups; serves 4 to 6

2 cups raw walnuts

2 celery stalks, coarsely chopped

½ red bell pepper, cored, seeded, and coarsely chopped

1 large scallion (white and light green parts only), coarsely chopped

1 teaspoon sea salt

18 crackers, for serving

In the bowl of a food processor, combine the walnuts, celery, bell pepper, scallions, and salt and blend until smooth. Transfer to a dish and serve with crackers.

tip *garden herb sun tea*

Call it sun tea or flavored water—one of my favorite summer drinks is this infusion of garden herbs. It's a little different every time because I combine whatever I find in my garden—and I love them all! I grow thyme, mint, lemon balm, parsley, basil, dill, rosemary, and fennel, and all of them can go into this drink.

I pick a variety of leaves, chop them finely, mix them with water in a pitcher, and let them steep in the sun all day. I also love to add grated orange or lemon peel and spices like cinnamon and nutmeg. Play around with your own combinations; it's a refreshing change from water and you get health benefits from the herbs and spices.

Eggplant Bruschetta

If you are looking to decrease your consumption of bread and gluten, this is a fantastic alternative to traditional bruschetta. What I love about this dish is that it is so hearty and filling. Eggplant has the ability to stand in for the toast in bruschetta because it holds its shape and has a mild flavor, so it allows the taste of the topping to shine through.

serves 4

2 medium eggplants

Sea salt and freshly ground black pepper

3 tablespoons olive oil

2 medium tomatoes, cored and chopped

½ small yellow onion, chopped

10 fresh basil leaves, finely chopped (about ½ cup)

1 teaspoon balsamic vinegar, plus more for serving

Garlic salt

½ cup feta cheese (optional)

1. Cut off the ends of the eggplants and peel them. Slice into ¼-inch-thick rounds, arrange the rounds in a baking dish, and sprinkle them with sea salt. Let sit for 20 minutes.
2. In a small bowl, combine 2 tablespoons of the olive oil, the tomatoes, onion, basil, and vinegar. Season with sea salt and pepper to taste and toss well. Set aside.
3. Gently rinse the eggplant slices under cold running water and pat dry. Heat the remaining 1 tablespoon olive oil in a skillet set over low heat. Add the eggplant slices and cook until the eggplant is brown and soft, about 7 minutes per side. Transfer the eggplant rounds to a serving platter and season with garlic salt to taste. Top with the tomato mixture, and sprinkle with the balsamic vinegar and feta cheese. Serve warm.

Lemon Dill Potato Salad

I have to say that my mom makes the best potato salad ever—a recipe that she learned from my grandma Otten, who worked as a governess for a wealthy family instead of going to high school. Grandma may not have been book educated, but boy was she smart and talented, especially in the kitchen. Mom and Grandma's salad is wonderful, but like many potato salads today, it is usually made with store-bought mayonnaise and mustard. What makes my recipe so delicious and better than ever is using homemade mayonnaise or Greek yogurt. It is also a beautiful dish to serve because it is so colorful, much more inviting than the bland potato salad at the store.

serves 4 to 5

1½ pounds red potatoes, cut into ½-inch pieces

2 cups petite green beans, cut into 2-inch pieces, or pickled green beans (page 53)

2 tablespoons fresh lemon juice

2 teaspoons olive oil

2 tablespoons chopped fresh dill

½ teaspoon sea salt

¼ teaspoon freshly ground black pepper

3 celery stalks, thinly sliced

5 radishes, thinly sliced

⅓ cup finely chopped red onion

½ cup Homemade Mayonnaise (see Tip) or plain Greek yogurt

1. Put the potatoes in a medium saucepan and cover with cold water. Bring to a boil over high heat, reduce the heat to medium low, and cook until the potatoes fall apart when pressed, about 7 minutes. Drain well and set aside.

2. Fill a medium saucepan with water and bring to a boil over high heat. Add the green beans and return to a boil. Cook until the green beans are just tender, about 2 minutes. Drain under cool running water. (Skip this step if you use pickled green beans.) Refrigerate.

3. In a medium bowl, whisk together the lemon juice, oil, dill, salt, and pepper. Add the potatoes, toss gently, cover, and refrigerate until chilled, about 45 minutes.

4. Add the green beans, celery, radishes, onion, and mayonnaise and stir well. Serve chilled.

tip *homemade mayonnaise*

I always avoided mayonnaise in the past because I knew that it—like many other store-bought foods—wasn't healthy. But once I started making my own, I began to enjoy it again.

Homemade mayonnaise is healthier and much more delicious, and it's incredibly easy. I will never go back to the store-bought stuff because I can control how tangy and spicy my own is. There are vegan recipes for mayonnaise, and I've tried them out. It is possible to make a tasty one, but I am too used to the taste of the egg yolk in mayonnaise to give it up.

makes about 1 cup

4 large organic egg yolks

2 teaspoons fresh lemon juice

2 teaspoons white vinegar

1 teaspoon ground mustard

⅛ teaspoon sea salt

1 cup grapeseed oil

In a food processor, combine the egg yolks, lemon juice, vinegar, ground mustard, and salt. With the blade running, slowly drizzle in the oil over a period of 3 to 4 minutes. The mayonnaise is ready when it is thick and creamy. It will keep in an airtight container in the refrigerator for up to 1 week.

Red Chard *with* Sweet Peppers *and* Tofu

I don't cook often with tofu, but I find that it works well in a stir-fry that has a great sauce. Tofu absorbs the flavors of the dish really nicely, so for this one I cook it after all the peppers and chard have had their turn in the pan. Red Swiss chard is one of the most beautiful vegetables to cook with and it's plentiful throughout the fall and winter. It also provides a plethora of antioxidants and has anti-inflammatory and detoxifying characteristics. I like to serve this dish with brown basmati rice.

serves 4

¼ cup grapeseed oil

1 red bell pepper, cored, seeded, and sliced

1 yellow bell pepper, cored, seeded, and sliced

1 bunch red chard, tough stems removed and coarsely chopped

1 (14-ounce) package extra-firm tofu, cut into ¾-inch sticks

3 tablespoons tamari or soy sauce

2 teaspoons sesame oil

Black and white sesame seeds, for garnish

1. Heat 1 tablespoon of the grapeseed oil in a large skillet set over medium-high heat. Add the peppers and cook until slightly soft, about 5 minutes. Transfer to a platter and cover loosely to keep warm.
2. Put the chard in the pan and cook, stirring, until wilted, 2 to 3 minutes. Transfer to the platter with the peppers and cover to keep warm.
3. Heat the remaining 3 tablespoons grapeseed oil in the skillet. Working in batches, fry the tofu until golden brown on all sides, about 1 minute per side. Using a slotted spoon, transfer the tofu to the platter with the peppers and chard.
4. Add the tamari and sesame oil to the skillet, swirling to combine. Pour the sauce over the tofu and peppers. Garnish with the sesame seeds and serve hot.

Coconut Boysenberry Smoothie

This smoothie is for the dog days of summer when you don't want to turn anything on that will create heat. The simplicity of this recipe allows you to interchange other fruits (blackberries, raspberries, strawberries, peaches) for the boysenberries and have delightful results every time. I like to think of it as a liquid Pure Bar because it tastes like a dessert but is healthy and nutritious—just like the bars!

serves 4

1 (13.5-ounce) can coconut milk

½ cup almond milk, homemade (page 34) or store-bought

1 teaspoon vanilla extract

3 tablespoons agave nectar

1 cup boysenberries

1 frozen banana

⅛ teaspoon sea salt

In a blender, combine the coconut milk, almond milk, vanilla, agave, boysenberries, banana, and salt and purée until smooth. Serve immediately.

Frozen Sugared Limes

Have you longed for a dessert that everyone will love to eat—especially kids—*and* is very high in antioxidants? What better dessert to give them than straight fruit with just a little organic sugar. My family and I discovered this easy dessert while in Mexico with some friends. My kids think they taste like sour candy—like those gummy ones you find at the supermarket. You can be proud to serve this "candy" to anyone!

serves 4 to 6

6 tablespoons organic cane sugar

4 limes, thinly sliced

1. Put the sugar in the bowl of a food processor and pulse until it is a fine powder, 30 to 45 seconds. Let sit for 1 minute to settle.
2. Pour the fine sugar into a small bowl and toss the limes until both sides are covered with sugar. Arrange the lime slices in a single layer on a plate and freeze for 1 hour. Store in an airtight container in the freezer for up to 1 week.

tip *waste-free lunch*

Yes, a waste-free lunch is truly possible! Before plastic was invented (it wasn't mass-produced until the 1940s) and before paper packaging was widely used, my grandparents used to wrap sandwiches and snacks in cloth. Grandma talks about how when she walked to school in the winter, they would put hot baked potatoes that were on the stove all night in their pockets to keep them warm as they walked and then eat them for lunch. How beautifully simple!

Today there are very clever ways to pack waste free:

- Select a reusable lunch bag.
- Select a reusable stainless-steel water or juice container.
- Buy more food in bulk and use a little at a time in containers you already have.
- Wrap sandwiches and snacks in cloth. Tie shut with twine, if necessary.
- Buy biodegradable sandwich bags for sandwiches and snacks.
- Use containers you already have and can wash.
- Wash and reuse your plastic zip-top bags and bread bags.

Peach Raspberry Crostata

This is one of those recipes that's perfect for a Saturday morning when you can go to the farmer's market, tote your bounty home, roll up your sleeves, and cook something amazing! It is definitely more involved than other dishes, but it's totally worth it. This is also a great recipe to make with your kids because it teaches them some basic cooking skills like making dough and peeling peaches.

This dough is versatile and can be used for any sweet or savory pie, tart, quiche, or turnover. You can even make the dough into cookies, sprinkling sugar on the tops before baking. It's a great recipe to know, so get creative with it! Here, the end result is an impressive, delicious tart that tastes like summer.

serves 4 to 6

DOUGH

1¼ cups white whole-wheat flour

2 teaspoons organic confectioners' sugar

¼ teaspoon sea salt

½ cup (1 stick) unsalted butter, chilled and cut into small pieces

3 tablespoons cold water

FILLING

3 medium (or 2 large) ripe peaches

6 tablespoons organic granulated sugar

¼ cup white whole-wheat flour, plus more for dusting

3 tablespoons salted butter, at room temperature

¼ teaspoon ground cinnamon

1 teaspoon vanilla extract

⅔ cup raspberries

1. For the dough, in the bowl of a food processor, combine the flour, confectioners' sugar, and salt. Pulse 2 or 3 times. Add the butter and pulse until partially combined, 3 or 4 times. Drizzle the water over the mixture and pulse until the dough comes together in several pieces.
2. Turn the dough out onto a work surface, form it into a ball, and then flatten into a 1-inch-thick disk. Wrap tightly in plastic wrap and refrigerate for 15 minutes. The dough can be refrigerated for up to 5 days or frozen for up to 2 months.
3. Preheat the oven to 325°F. Line a baking sheet with parchment paper.

4. For the filling, bring a small pot of water to a boil over high heat. Score a small "X" in the bottom of each peach and put them into the boiling water for 20 seconds. Remove the peaches from the water and put them under cold running water until cool enough to handle. Starting at the "X," peel the skins from the peaches and discard. Slice the peaches and put them in a small bowl. Stir in 2 tablespoons of the granulated sugar and set aside.

5. Put the flour, remaining 4 tablespoons granulated sugar, butter, cinnamon, and vanilla in a medium bowl. Using your fingers, rub the mixture together until it resembles a coarse meal. Set aside.

6. Dust a clean work surface with flour. Roll the chilled dough out into a circle about 12 inches across. Transfer the dough to the prepared baking sheet. Spread half of the flour filling mixture on the bottom of the crust, leaving a 2-inch border. Arrange half of the peaches and half of the raspberries over the flour mixture. Scatter the remaining flour mixture over the peaches, and put the remaining peaches and raspberries on top. Fold the edges of the dough over the filling to make a 2-inch border and pinch to flatten.

7. Bake until the crust is golden brown and the filling is bubbly, about 50 minutes. Let cool on a wire rack for 10 minutes before slicing. Serve hot, warm, or at room temperature.

september

Raspberry Pancakes

Cantaloupe Ginger Salad

Roasted Butternut Squash and Apple Bisque

Endive, Escarole, and Golden Beet Salad

Heirloom Tomato and Walnut Pesto Wrap

Cilantro Lime Buckwheat

Eggplant Love Lasagne

Pasta alla Checca

Blackberry Crisp

Rum-Roasted Fruit

I think that September is ***my favorite month*** in Michigan. The summer is still hanging on, but the nights are cooler and the angle of the sun casts a breathtaking sheen on the lush landscape. Everything is green and mature and healthy. ***The days are more peaceful***, not just because school has started but also because summer hustle and bustle has turned into fall focus. There is more quiet time for reflection.

In Michigan there is a cultural shift toward fall in September. The apple orchards start to get busier, with hayrides, fresh homemade doughnuts, and animals for the kids to pet. The local wineries have events to celebrate the harvest and wine making. There is an anticipation of the cool weather and fall traditions, yet it is still warm and sunny.

The harvest is so strong around us this time of year that ***preservation is a wonderful skill to have.*** There is so much fresh food that you couldn't possibly eat it in one month. My favorite ways of preserving are making freezer jam (page 102), drying my own herbs (page 180), and pickling vegetables (page 53) and happen to be the easiest, too. I love to make my own salsa and guacamole with the fresh vegetables. Cold soups and smoothies with farmer's market veggies are always in the kitchen, along with seasonal favorites using raspberries, apples, squash, and cantaloupe.

SEPTEMBER

Here is a sample menu I've put together with
a variety of recipes for this month.

breakfast

Raspberry Pancakes

•

lunch

Cilantro Lime Buckwheat

•

midday snack

Cantaloupe Ginger Salad

•

dinner

Eggplant Love Lasagne

•

dessert

Blackberry Crisp

Raspberry Pancakes

Imagine this: It's Saturday morning and everyone else is still sleeping. You walk outside into a quiet morning with birds singing and a slow, cool morning breeze. Around the corner of your house is a raspberry bush that is heavy with fruit. You pick a bowlful of big juicy raspberries, sneaking a few succulent morsels because you can't help it. You head back inside to make raspberry pancakes from scratch for the family.

This fantasy can come true even if you don't have a raspberry bush at your house. I love this pancake recipe because you can use any kind of fruit, or even go fruitless! The house begins to fill with wonderful smells of wholesome food. What a great way to start a Saturday!

serves 4 to 6

2¼ cups white whole-wheat flour

2 teaspoons baking powder

½ teaspoon sea salt

2 cups almond milk, homemade (page 34) or store-bought

4 large eggs, separated

Zest and segments from 1 orange

1 tablespoon organic cane sugar

4 teaspoons grapeseed oil

2 (6-ounce) containers fresh raspberries

Honey or maple syrup, for serving (optional)

1. In a large bowl, whisk together the flour, baking powder, and salt.
2. In a small bowl, whisk together the almond milk, egg yolks, and orange zest. Pour into the flour mixture and stir just until combined.
3. In the bowl of an electric mixer fitted with the whisk attachment, beat the egg whites on medium speed until foamy, about 2 minutes. Sprinkle in the sugar and beat until stiff peaks form, about 5 minutes. Gently fold the egg whites into the batter.
4. Heat a large nonstick skillet over medium-high heat. Brush with some of the oil. Pour ½ cup of batter onto the skillet for each pancake. Scatter a few raspberries on top and cook until bubbles begin to appear around the edges of the pancake, about 2 minutes. Flip and cook until cooked through, 1 to 2 more minutes. Repeat with the remaining batter.
5. Serve the pancakes hot with the orange segments and remaining raspberries, and drizzled with the honey.

Cantaloupe Ginger Salad

Cantaloupes are very easy to grow, and they're also on the list of the "clean 15," which means they are not often found to be contaminated with pesticides even if they are not grown organically. Have you ever picked a ripe cantaloupe right from your garden? If not, try growing some next season. We've easily grown them from the seeds of juicy farmer's market melons in the past.

It's almost difficult for me to make a recipe out of a ripe cantaloupe. They are so delicious on their own! But this combination of sweet cantaloupe, blueberries, and ginger dressing is sweet, a touch spicy, and wonderfully refreshing. I like to serve this cantaloupe blueberry dish for dessert topped with coconut ice cream.

serves 4

1 ripe cantaloupe
1 cup fresh blueberries
2 tablespoons fresh lime juice
1 tablespoon honey
¼ teaspoon ground ginger
⅛ teaspoon sea salt
1 teaspoon grated fresh ginger

1. Halve and seed the cantaloupe, and then, using a melon baller, scoop balls of fruit out of the flesh. Put the melon balls and blueberries in a serving bowl.
2. In a small bowl, whisk together the lime juice, honey, ground ginger, and salt. Pour the dressing over the fruit and toss gently. Add the grated ginger and stir gently. Serve immediately or chill before serving.

tip ways to use less gas

- **LIVE WITHIN YOUR NEIGHBORHOOD.** Find activities that are close to home and enjoy them.
- **WALK, SKATEBOARD, AND RIDE BIKES.** You don't have to drive just a few blocks away to a friend's house or the tennis courts.
- **DRIVE SMART.** Don't accelerate so fast after stops, brake less, coast more, anticipate light changes ahead, and turn off the AC.
- **EAT MORE MEALS AT HOME.** Save a driving trip to a restaurant!

Roasted Butternut Squash *and* Apple Bisque

If we're lucky, we can start picking apples mid-September. There is a locally owned organic apple farm about 20 miles away where we can get pesticide-free apples right off the tree. To me, an apple off the tree is completely different from a store-bought apple that probably sat in a warehouse for months and months.

My kids would drink this soup with a straw if I let them. Roasting the vegetables brings out their sweetness, and the almond milk increases the soup's richness while keeping it vegan. I also try to buy cubed organic butternut squash, if I can find it, because it cuts down on the prep time. But if that is not available, the easiest way to cut up a butternut squash is to cut off both ends, making each end a flat surface, cut the "neck" off the "body," and then run your knife or vegetable peeler carefully down the sides. Then simply cut in half, scoop out the seeds, and chop it.

serves 4

1 large butternut squash, chopped (about 3 cups)

3 medium apples, cored and coarsely chopped

1 medium yellow onion, cut into 8 wedges

1 teaspoon fresh thyme leaves, plus more for garnish

2 teaspoons chopped fresh sage

½ teaspoon sea salt

¼ teaspoon freshly ground black pepper

¼ cup grapeseed oil

2 cups almond milk, homemade (page 34) or store-bought, warmed

1. Preheat the oven to 400°F. Line a baking sheet with foil.
2. In a large bowl, combine the butternut squash, apples, onion, thyme, sage, salt, and pepper. Drizzle the grapeseed oil over the top and toss well. Transfer to the prepared baking sheet.
3. Roast until golden brown, 40 to 45 minutes. Let cool for 5 minutes.
4. Transfer the vegetables to the work bowl of a food processor and process until smooth. Add the almond milk and pulse until the desired consistency is reached. Garnish with fresh thyme and serve hot.

Endive, Escarole, *and* Golden Beet Salad

Endive and escarole are unique greens that make any dish just a little more gourmet and impressive. They come from the root of chicory and have a hearty, slightly bitter taste that blends well with creamy and spicy ingredients. They are loaded with important vitamins like K, B, and C, and minerals like calcium, iron, magnesium, and folate.

This savory salad is easy to whip together, and most of the ingredients are available at your local farmer's market. I especially love endive leaves because they form a cup and can be used as such. I often fill them with hummus (page 37) or a vegan pâté like my Walnut Pâté (page 148) or pesto (page 166). You can even fill them with chopped fruit and drizzle with honey. They are definitely fun, versatile, and interesting to serve, like nature's little chips.

serves 4 to 6

3 medium golden beets, greens and roots removed

3 tablespoons plain yogurt or plain coconut yogurt for vegan

1 tablespoon rice vinegar

1 tablespoon olive oil

1 teaspoon fresh lemon juice

1½ teaspoons fresh thyme leaves

½ teaspoon chopped garlic

¼ teaspoon sea salt

⅛ teaspoon freshly ground black pepper

1 head endive

1 head escarole, tough outer leaves removed

Thyme or chive flowers, for garnish

1. Preheat the oven to 425°F.
2. Wrap the beets in foil and put them on a baking sheet. Roast until they begin to soften, about 45 minutes. Remove the pan from the oven and let stand at room temperature until cool enough to handle. Remove the skins from the beets (they should slip right off) and cut the beets in half lengthwise. Slice ¼ inch thick and set aside.
3. Meanwhile, in the bowl of a food processor, combine the yogurt, vinegar, oil, lemon juice, thyme, garlic, salt, and pepper. Blend until smooth. Set aside.
4. Cut 1 inch off the root ends of both the endive and the escarole. Chop the escarole and divide it among salad plates. Arrange the endive leaves and beets on top. Drizzle with the dressing, garnish with the thyme flowers, and serve immediately.

Heirloom Tomato *and* Walnut Pesto Wrap

I'm a sucker for pesto of all kinds. The beautiful thing with this recipe is that it's a vegan pesto that delivers all the flavor of a regular pesto but with super-healthy ingredients. It is so good for you that you can have it whenever you want, and I often end up eating spoonfuls of this before it even gets to the sandwich! Because walnuts are less expensive than pine nuts, they are a good stand-in for pesto. This is my Sunday evening special—you know, the casual supper that you can eat in the den. I like to serve this sandwich with soup and cut-up fruit.

serves 4

PESTO

1 avocado, peeled, pitted, and chopped

1½ cups fresh basil leaves

½ cup fresh oregano leaves

½ cup walnuts

1 garlic clove

½ teaspoon tamari or soy sauce

4 (6-inch) flour tortillas

2 ripe tomatoes, sliced

1 cup baby spinach

1. For the pesto, in the bowl of a food processor, combine the avocado, basil, oregano, walnuts, garlic, and tamari and purée until smooth.
2. Spread the pesto on the tortillas, layer with tomato and spinach, and roll into wraps.

Cilantro Lime Buckwheat

Although there are people who don't care for the flavor of cilantro, I think it tastes like summer. I wonder whether people's aversion may be due to the fact that the herb is sometimes an overpowering presence in a dish. The key with cilantro is to blend it well so it doesn't stand out from the other ingredients, and then you have its light, delicious taste. I love pairing it with buckwheat for this salad because it is a unique flavor combination. Buckwheat has a very hearty and earthy flavor that meshes really well with the lime, ginger, and cilantro. It's like a salsa with some oomph! I prefer this dish as a cold salad, served on the porch with cut-up fruit or gazpacho.

serves 4

2 cups filtered water

1 cup buckwheat

3 tablespoons olive oil

2 tablespoons fresh lime juice

1 teaspoon grated fresh ginger

¾ teaspoon sea salt

¼ teaspoon freshly ground black pepper

½ cup chopped fresh cilantro leaves

4 scallions, sliced (white and light green parts only)

2 medium tomatoes, chopped, for garnish

1. Bring the water to a boil in a medium saucepan set over high heat. Rinse the buckwheat under cool running water and add it to the boiling water. Cover the pan, reduce the heat to medium-low, and simmer until soft, about 20 minutes. Remove the pan from the heat and let stand, covered, for 5 minutes.

2. In a medium bowl, whisk together the oil, lime juice, ginger, salt, and pepper. Add the cooked buckwheat and mix well. Stir in the cilantro and scallions. Garnish with the tomatoes and serve hot, at room temperature, or chilled.

Eggplant Love Lasagne

This fresh, simple, and gluten-free lasagne is perfect for a romantic night in. Eggplant is a wonderful vegetable to use in dishes instead of meat because it is hearty and flavorful and takes on other seasonings well. It's also rich in phytonutrients, which protect our bodies from cell damage that can lead to disease. There's no pasta to weigh you down, and granulated tapioca soaks up the juices from the vegetables. For an extra-special presentation, bake these in four individual gratin dishes.

serves 4

1 tablespoon extra-virgin olive oil

2 tablespoons granulated tapioca

1 large eggplant, peeled and thinly sliced

Sea salt and freshly ground black pepper

1 cup Avocado Pesto (page 89) or store-bought pesto

½ cup jarred roasted red bell pepper, rinsed, patted dry, and coarsely chopped

1 cup ricotta cheese

4 ounces mozzarella cheese, grated (1 cup)

2 medium tomatoes, cored and thinly sliced

4 ounces mozzarella cheese, thinly sliced

1. Preheat the oven to 375°F.
2. Drizzle the olive oil in the bottom of a 9 × 9-inch baking dish. Sprinkle in the tapioca. Cover the bottom of the dish with one layer of eggplant slices. Sprinkle with salt and pepper. Spread half of the pesto over the eggplant and top with the roasted red bell pepper.
3. In a small bowl, season the ricotta cheese with salt and pepper and stir in the grated mozzarella cheese. Spoon the cheese mixture over the red bell pepper layer. Make another layer of eggplant slices on top of the ricotta mixture. Spread with the remaining pesto. Top with the tomato slices, and then the mozzarella slices. Season with salt and pepper.
4. Bake until the lasagne is heated through and the top is beginning to brown, 30 to 35 minutes. Let cool for 15 minutes before serving.

Pasta alla Checca

When I get perfect tomatoes, splendid fragrant basil, and sweet garlic from my garden or the market, I feel like cooking them is almost a shame. There are times when food is so perfect, it just needs to be eaten raw. And besides, there's nothing easier! Pasta alla checca is a traditional Italian dish that is too delicious this time of year not to make. It takes less than 30 minutes and is bursting with the freshest and healthiest ingredients around. It's a staple for us and is beautiful when paired with a rich whole-wheat or other grain pasta.

serves 4

1 (12-ounce) package brown rice spaghetti

3 tablespoons olive oil

9 Roma or heirloom tomatoes, cored and chopped

3 garlic cloves, chopped

½ cup chopped fresh basil leaves

½ teaspoon sea salt

1. Cook the spaghetti in a large saucepan of boiling water until al dente, about 8 minutes or according to the package directions. Drain and toss with 1 tablespoon of the olive oil.

2. In a large bowl, combine the tomatoes, garlic, basil, salt, and remaining 2 tablespoons oil. Add the spaghetti and toss well. Serve hot.

Blackberry Crisp

Blackberries off the vine are a treat in Michigan. In my experience, wild blackberries are significantly different from store-bought, so if you can get your hands on local blackberries this time of year, don't hesitate!

When I was a camp counselor we used to take the kids out to a thicket of blackberries and fill our buckets with them. I always wonder how many bugs one consumes while picking berries because you can hardly help but pop them in your mouth one after another! If you can find the self-control to wait and make this fantastic blackberry crisp, it will definitely be worth it, and you will probably consume far fewer bugs.

serves 6 to 8

1 tablespoon unsalted butter or vegan buttery spread, for greasing

FILLING

2/3 cup organic cane sugar

1/4 cup granulated tapioca

1/8 teaspoon grated nutmeg

4 cups fresh blackberries

2 tablespoons fresh orange juice

2 teaspoons grated orange zest

TOPPING

1/2 cup quick-cooking oats

1/3 cup packed organic light brown sugar

1/4 cup coconut flour

1/4 cup almond meal

1/8 teaspoon grated nutmeg

1/4 cup (1/2 stick) unsalted butter or vegan buttery spread, at room temperature

1. Preheat the oven to 325°F. Grease a 9 × 9-inch baking dish with 1 tablespoon of the butter.

2. For the filling, in a medium bowl, combine the cane sugar, tapioca, and nutmeg. Add the blackberries, orange juice, and orange zest and toss well. Pour the mixture into the prepared baking dish.

3. For the topping, in a medium bowl, combine the oats, brown sugar, coconut flour, almond meal, and nutmeg. Add the butter and, using your fingers, blend it in. Sprinkle the topping evenly over the fruit filling.

4. Bake until the top begins to brown and the filling is bubbly and thick, about 45 minutes. Cover loosely with foil if the top starts to get too brown. Serve hot, warm, or at room temperature.

Rum-Roasted Fruit

This recipe came about because I had half a bottle of Sailor Jerry Spiced Rum in the freezer left after making vegan eggnog the prior holiday season. I knew I wouldn't drink it (I'm much more of a wine girl), and it was taking up valuable freezer space, so I created a recipe with it. At the time, I had apples and cranberries in the house, which I originally used in the recipe. I subsequently made it with raspberries when they were in season instead of cranberries and actually liked it even more! I am excited to try this recipe with pears as well as peaches and blueberries.

The key to roasting fruit for this dish is to cover it at first and let it get all bubbly and soft, then uncover and caramelize it at high heat. You want the fruit to be soft but also slightly browned on the edges for the best flavor! Serve it in small bowls topped with yogurt, coconut ice cream, or homemade almond milk. Is your mouth watering yet?

serves 2

3 tablespoons Sailor Jerry Spiced Rum

2 tablespoons honey

½ teaspoon vanilla extract

¼ teaspoon ground cinnamon

¼ teaspoon ground nutmeg

2 cups chopped apples, such as Fuji or Gala

1 cup fresh raspberries

1. Preheat the oven to 400°F.
2. In a medium bowl, whisk together the rum, honey, vanilla, cinnamon, and nutmeg. Add the apples and raspberries and stir to coat. Pour the mixture into a pie dish and cover with foil.
3. Bake until the fruit is soft and bubbly, about 20 minutes. Increase the oven temperature to 450°F. Uncover the dish and bake until the fruit is browned on the edges, about 7 more minutes. Serve warm.

october

Apple Walnut French Toast

Italian Egg White Scramble

Pear and Spinach Salad with Maple Pecans

Cranberry Leek Quinoa

Stuffed Cabbage Rolls with Fresh Tomato Sauce

Pasta in Pumpkin Sauce

Red Lentil Cumin Soup

Twice-Baked Yams

Gluten-Free Lemon Poppy Seed Cupcakes

Stewed Apples

Michigan has a spectacular fall season (except for one year when it snowed on October 1). There are so many different species of trees here in Michigan that the colors are diverse and brilliant. The ***cooler weather is often a welcome*** change from the hot, humid days of summer, and everyone is simply happy to be alive!

It is the time of year for apple orchards, vineyard visits, wine tasting, hayrides, homemade doughnuts, cider mills, and bountiful farmer's markets with apples, pears, pumpkins, melons, cabbage, and brilliant colored peppers.

Do you ever stop to think of the many generations before us who have enjoyed and appreciated fall? I remember being in the kitchen making homemade applesauce with my mother and grandmother just as they did years before with their parents and grandparents. Generations of people have experienced the brilliance of creation and loved the bounty of the harvest. Fall is a ***time of thanksgiving*** and reflection on months of spring renewal and summer fun. Fall is the last hurrah, the going-away party, the "savor every last morsel" season, and it is truly lovely.

OCTOBER

Here is a sample menu I've put together with
a variety of recipes for this month.

breakfast

Apple Walnut French Toast

•

lunch

Red Lentil Cumin Soup

•

midday snack

Gluten-Free Lemon Poppy Seed Cupcakes

•

dinner

Pasta in Pumpkin Sauce

•

dessert

Stewed Apples

Apple Walnut French Toast

This is the best breakfast for that first crisp, cool, almost chilly fall morning. The aroma of it cooking makes me think of playing football in the yard with the family, or hiking through the fall leaves.

Forget going out for brunch; instead make this and the Italian Egg White Scramble (page 178), call some friends, and have them over for a fun, casual weekend meal.

serves 4

2 tablespoons (¼ stick) unsalted butter

1 green apple, peeled, cored, and thinly sliced

¼ cup maple syrup

1½ teaspoons ground cinnamon

2 large eggs

½ cup almond milk, homemade (page 34) or store-bought

2 tablespoons agave nectar

½ teaspoon walnut extract

4 thick bread slices, such as sourdough

⅓ cup walnut halves

1. Melt 1 tablespoon of the butter in a medium nonstick skillet set over medium heat. Add the apples, maple syrup, and ½ teaspoon of the cinnamon, and cook, stirring occasionally, until the apples are soft, about 5 minutes. Remove the pan from the heat and set aside.
2. In a medium bowl, whisk together the eggs, almond milk, agave, walnut extract, and remaining 1 teaspoon cinnamon. Dip each bread slice into the egg mixture, coating each side well.
3. Heat the remaining 1 tablespoon butter in a large nonstick skillet set over medium-high heat. Put the bread slices in the pan and cook until golden brown, 2 to 3 minutes. Flip the slices and cook until cooked through, about 2 more minutes.
4. Cut the slices in half, put 2 halves on each of 4 plates, and top with the apple mixture. Sprinkle with the walnuts and serve hot.

tip *the apple's dirty little secret*

Apple picking is a favorite fall activity in many parts of the United States, yet many people are not aware that apples are one of the most heavily sprayed fruits. The average conventionally grown apple has more than forty-eight different pesticides on it. Apples often occupy the top spot of the Environmental Working Group's infamous "Dirty Dozen" list of foods (the twelve most contaminated produce items), and it's always recommended to buy organic. Because apples are the third-most consumed fruit in the country, that's a lot of chemicals going into our bodies. These pesticides have been linked to Parkinson's disease and other nervous system problems and are suspected in causing reproductive problems, as well as leukemia. They also contaminate our soil and groundwater.

In my opinion, searching for a local, organic apple orchard is a must. It will be a treasure and provide you with apples that are not only clean but more flavorful. It is also great to teach your kids what real apples look like! And choosing organic apples will help create demand for organic farms, which leads to a cleaner earth for us all.

Italian Egg White Scramble

Breakfast and veggies are not synonymous to many people, but I have found that with the right combination of savory flavors, you may actually start to crave vegetables for breakfast instead of sugary sweet things. And although squash does not usually show up in eggs, you will be delighted at how delicious it is! In fact, there are so many colorful tastes going on in this dish that you won't miss the egg yolks—and maybe you'll decide to make it a dinner staple as well.

serves 4

1½ tablespoons olive oil

1 small zucchini, halved lengthwise and sliced

1 small yellow or crookneck squash, halved lengthwise and sliced

1 cup halved grape or cherry tomatoes

12 large egg whites

½ cup finely sliced fresh basil leaves

¼ teaspoon turmeric

Sea salt and freshly ground black pepper

Heat the oil in a large nonstick skillet set over medium heat. Add the zucchini and squash and cook, stirring frequently, until soft, 3 to 4 minutes. Add the tomatoes and cook until soft, about 3 minutes. Pour in the egg whites, sprinkle with the basil and turmeric, and season with salt and pepper. Cook, stirring with a heatproof spatula, until the eggs are cooked through, 2 to 3 minutes. Serve immediately.

Pear and Spinach Salad with Maple Pecans

I'd really like to grow a pear tree someday. My neighbor planted the cutest little pear tree one year, and I will never forget the day that I walked by it and saw the first little fruit hanging delicately from a branch. I have wanted my own ever since.

Pears are a lifesaver in the fall and winter. In a season of fewer fresh fruits, they are a bright spot. I adore the creamy dressing in this salad, as well as the aroma of toasted pecans that fills the house. This salad is like a meal because it includes fruit, nuts, greens, and a hearty, healthy dressing: all the major food groups in my book!

serves 4 to 6

½ cup plain yogurt

3 tablespoons white balsamic vinegar

3 tablespoons chopped fresh flat-leaf parsley

¾ teaspoon sea salt

¾ cup whole pecans

1 tablespoon maple syrup

3 cups loosely packed baby spinach or 1 (6-ounce) package baby spinach

½ cup sliced red onion

2 Anjou pears, cored and thinly sliced

1. In the bowl of a food processor or blender, combine the yogurt, vinegar, parsley, and salt and process until smooth. Set aside.
2. Put the pecans in a small skillet set over medium heat and cook, stirring occasionally, until aromatic and lightly toasted, about 2 minutes. Remove the pan from the heat and stir in the maple syrup. Set aside.
3. To serve, arrange the spinach, onion, and pears on serving plates. Drizzle with the dressing and top with the maple pecans. Serve immediately.

tip *dry your own herbs*

Drying your own herbs is a wonderful way to preserve what you've grown while saving money at the same time. To dry herbs, place fresh herb leaves (like thyme, basil, mint, or rosemary) in a single layer on a baking sheet. Dry in an oven set to 110°F. If your oven doesn't get that low, put it on its lowest setting and prop the oven door open with a wooden spoon. Let the herbs slowly dehydrate all day.

Different herbs take different amounts of time to fully dry depending on the thickness of the leaf. Check them every hour or so until they are dry and crumbly, but not burnt. This is a great activity to do on a cool spring day. Your entire house will smell amazing! I store my dried herbs in my spice cupboard in small spice or jam jars that I have saved. I try to use them within a year for optimal flavor.

Cranberry Leek Quinoa

When I start to see fresh organic cranberries pop up in the grocery store, I buy as many bags as I can fit in my freezer. I love cooking with fresh cranberries and freeze them so that I can make my cranberry dishes all year. My kids devour my Curried Cranberry Sauce (page 204), which is a year-round staple in our house, as well as this wonderful grain dish. Quinoa has a fall feel to me, perhaps because its flavor is so nutty. Combined with squash and cranberries, this dish takes all the good smells and tastes of the season and makes them into a beautiful meal.

serves 4

2 cups filtered water

1 cup quinoa, rinsed and drained

1 tablespoon grapeseed oil

2 cups finely chopped butternut or acorn squash

2 leeks, white and pale green parts only, washed well and thinly sliced

1 tablespoon chopped fresh sage

1 cup cranberries

¼ cup chopped fresh flat-leaf parsley

1 tablespoon agave nectar or maple syrup

2 teaspoons fresh lemon juice

Sea salt and freshly ground black pepper

1. In a medium saucepan set over high heat, bring the water and quinoa to a boil. Cover, reduce the heat to low, and cook until the water has been absorbed, about 15 minutes. Set aside.

2. Heat the oil in a large skillet set over medium-high heat. Add the squash and cook, stirring, until slightly softened, about 6 minutes. Add the leeks and sage and cook, stirring, until the squash is tender and the leeks are lightly golden, about 6 minutes. Add the cranberries and cook just until they start to pop, about 2 minutes. Stir in the parsley, agave, and lemon juice. Add the cooked quinoa and stir well. Season with salt and pepper and serve hot, warm, at room temperature, or cold.

Stuffed Cabbage Rolls *with* Fresh Tomato Sauce

My neighbor Fadi makes amazing stuffed grape leaves. When his mother visited the United States, she taught my kids how to make them. They were young at the time, but they have loved the dish ever since. It shows that when you get kids involved in making something, they are much more likely to give it a chance and not be nearly as scared to eat it or be critical.

This recipe is my version of stuffed grape leaves, using cabbage leaves instead, which are easier to find in my part of the world. I've found that if you freeze the cabbage leaves for an hour, and then thaw them a little before filling, they become soft and easier to work with while retaining their color (the color can be lost if you boil the leaves to soften them). I make it with and without the raisins, depending on my mood (and what's in the pantry).

serves 4

8 large napa cabbage leaves

1 cup brown rice

2¼ cups filtered water

1 tablespoon grapeseed oil

1 medium leek, white and pale green parts only, washed well and finely sliced

1 celery stalk, finely chopped

1 large carrot, finely chopped

2 teaspoons chopped fresh thyme leaves

½ teaspoon sea salt

¼ cup chopped walnuts

¼ cup golden raisins

1 tablespoon olive oil

½ cup coarsely chopped yellow onion

2 garlic cloves, coarsely chopped

2 large tomatoes, cored and coarsely chopped

⅓ cup vegetable broth, homemade (see Tip) or store-bought, or mushroom broth

1 teaspoon red wine vinegar

1. Put the cabbage leaves in the freezer for 1 hour.
2. Combine the rice and water in a medium saucepan set over high heat. Bring to a boil, cover, reduce the heat to low, and simmer until the rice is cooked, about 45 minutes.
3. Meanwhile, heat the grapeseed oil in a large skillet set over medium-high heat. Add the leek, celery, carrot, thyme, and ¼ teaspoon of the salt and cook, stirring, until lightly golden, about 5 minutes. Remove the pan from the heat and stir in the walnuts, raisins, and rice. Set the filling aside.
4. Heat the olive oil in a large skillet set over medium heat. Add the onion and cook, stirring, until softened, about 5 minutes. Add the garlic and tomatoes and cook, stirring, until the tomatoes begin to fall apart, about 3 minutes. Add the broth, vinegar, and remaining ¼ teaspoon salt and bring to a boil. Reduce the heat to low and simmer until the flavors meld, about 5 minutes. Set the sauce aside.

5. Preheat the oven to 350°F.

6. Remove the cabbage leaves from the freezer and let thaw for 10 minutes.

7. Cut out the tough center stem of the cabbage leaves, leaving the top half of the leaves intact. Overlap the cut center of the cabbage leaves and put ⅓ cup of the filling in the center of each leaf. Fold the sides of the leaf over and roll it up.

8. Spoon half the sauce into the bottom of a 9 × 9-inch square baking dish. Put the cabbage rolls in the pan on top of the sauce, and then spoon the remaining sauce over the top. Cover loosely with foil.

9. Bake until heated through, about 12 minutes. Serve hot.

tip don't ever buy vegetable broth again!

Save the skins of your onions, carrots, celery, leek greens—any vegetable—and boil them for your own veggie broth. Keep a bag in the freezer full of vegetable scraps and whatever veggies and herbs go limp in your fridge. When it is full, empty everything into a big pot, cover with water, and boil for an hour or so (salt is optional; I add it later when making soup). Strain the broth and freeze.

Pasta in Pumpkin Sauce

Sage and pumpkin are a match made in heaven, and if you can get either or both fresh from your own garden or the local farmer's market, well, even better! Sage is a beautiful, ornamental herb to grow. Common or broadleaf sage is the type most often used in cooking. It has soft, light green leaves and big purple flowers that bloom in late spring or early summer. Sage has been used in culinary and medicinal recipes for thousands of years and is one of the oldest and most widely used herbs. It has anti-inflammatory properties as well as antioxidants that prevent cell damage that can lead to disease. Studies have also shown sage to be a memory enhancer, great for busy moms whose brains are too full!

serves 4 to 6

1 pound whole-wheat pasta (shell or tube shaped)

2 tablespoons olive oil

2 leeks, white and pale green parts only, washed well and sliced

8 ounces wild mushrooms, sliced

1 (15-ounce) can pumpkin purée or 1¾ cups homemade purée (see Tip)

1 cup almond milk, homemade (page 34) or store-bought

1 tablespoon maple syrup

1 cup pine nuts

2 tablespoons coarsely chopped fresh sage leaves

¼ teaspoon sea salt, plus more to taste

Freshly ground black pepper

¼ cup freshly grated Parmesan cheese, for garnish (optional)

3 whole fresh sage leaves, for garnish (optional)

1. Cook the pasta in a large pot of boiling water until al dente, about 7 minutes or according to the package directions. Drain, return the pasta to the pot, and cover to keep warm.
2. Heat the oil in a large skillet set over medium-high heat. Add the leeks and cook, stirring, until softened, about 3 minutes. Add the mushrooms and cook, stirring, until lightly golden, about 5 minutes.
3. Meanwhile, in the bowl of a food processor, combine the pumpkin purée, almond milk, maple syrup, pine nuts, chopped sage, and ¼ teaspoon salt and pulse until blended. Add the pumpkin mixture to the skillet with the leeks and mushrooms and stir well. Cook, stirring, until warmed through, about 2 minutes. Season with salt and pepper. Pour the sauce into the pot with the cooked pasta and stir well.
4. Serve hot, garnished with the Parmesan and sage leaves.

tip *preparing your own pumpkin purée*

October marks the reappearance of everything pumpkin flavored, like pies, bars, veggie recipes, and more. Many delicious fall recipes call for pumpkin purée. Canned pumpkin on store shelves leads us to assume that it must be so difficult to make from scratch that we must resort to the can. Or maybe it's just a habit because we have always bought pumpkin in a can. Either way, you can easily cook and purée your own pumpkin just like you would any other squash, because in the end, pumpkin is just one *big* squash.

Choose a pumpkin that's small to medium sized. Although I typically go for the ugly pumpkins when carving jack-o'-lanterns because I feel sorry for them, when I cook, I go for the pretty ones. I think that the smaller, blemish-free pumpkins actually have the best flavor, and they're easier to handle.

Preheat the oven to 375°F. Cut off the top of the pumpkin, cut it in half and then quarters, and scoop out the seeds like you would any squash. I use a large spoon and sometimes a paring knife to get the insides nice and clean. Save the seeds for roasting later, and place the quarters flesh-side up on a rimmed baking sheet. Bake until the pumpkin is soft, 1 hour. Let cool until it's cool enough to handle. Scoop the flesh into the bowl of a food processor, discard the skins, and blend until smooth. Use this purée as you would any pumpkin in a can. When you taste how pure and unadulterated this pumpkin flavor is, you will never go back!

Red Lentil Cumin Soup

Cumin is a polarizing ingredient for me. I like it only as a hint, and with certain other ingredients. When done right, it's just delicious—especially in the cooler months, because it's such a warm, heady spice. It's also a very healthy spice for women because it's a good source of both iron and calcium. But don't feel left out, guys—it is rumored to also be a strong aphrodisiac. This may have just become your favorite soup!

serves 4 to 6

1 tablespoon grapeseed oil

1 medium yellow onion, chopped

1 large carrot, chopped

2 celery stalks, chopped

2 garlic cloves, minced

1 teaspoon ground cumin

⅛ teaspoon ground ginger

7 cups vegetable broth, homemade (see Tip, page 183) or store-bought, or mushroom broth

½ teaspoon sea salt, plus more to taste

¼ teaspoon freshly ground black pepper, plus more to taste

1 pound red lentils, rinsed

2 medium tomatoes, cored and chopped

1. Heat the oil in a large saucepan set over medium-high heat. Add the onion and cook, stirring, until softened, about 4 minutes. Add the carrot and celery and cook, stirring, for 3 minutes. Stir in the garlic, cumin, and ginger, and cook for 1 more minute.
2. Add the broth, salt, pepper, lentils, and tomatoes. Raise the heat to high and bring to a boil. Reduce the heat to low and simmer until the lentils are soft, about 25 minutes.
3. Season to taste with salt and pepper and serve hot.

Twice-Baked Yams

Yams are God's gift to vegetarians. Hearty and full of flavor, yams are high in potassium and vitamin B6, both important for heart health. A serving also provides more than 20 percent of the daily recommended amount of vitamin C. They will forever remind me of fall family dinners and the big gathering next month, Thanksgiving. When yams are paired with the right spices, the flavor of these wonderful roots is unsurpassed. I hope this recipe will persuade you to never again put a marshmallow on such a beautiful food item!

serves 4

4 small yams

2 teaspoons grapeseed oil

3 tablespoons fresh orange juice

1 tablespoon coconut oil

3/8 teaspoon sea salt

3 tablespoons maple syrup

1/4 cup coarsely chopped hazelnuts

1. Preheat the oven to 375°F. Line a small baking dish with foil.
2. Pierce each yam with a knife and rub the skins with the oil. Put the yams in the prepared baking dish and bake until the flesh gives when pressed, about 40 minutes. Let cool until cool enough to handle.
3. Cutting lengthwise, slice off 1/2 inch from the side of each yam. Using a melon baller or spoon, scoop the flesh into a bowl, leaving 1/4 inch next to the skin intact, forming a shell. Put the skins back into the baking dish.
4. Put the yam flesh in the bowl of a food processor. Add the orange juice, coconut oil, 1/4 teaspoon of the salt, and 2 tablespoons of the maple syrup and blend until smooth. Spoon the mixture back into the yam skins.
5. In a small bowl, combine the remaining 1/8 teaspoon salt, remaining 1 tablespoon maple syrup, and the hazelnuts. Sprinkle the mixture over the tops of the yams.
6. Bake until the topping is lightly browned and the filling is heated through, about 15 minutes. Serve hot.

Gluten-Free Lemon Poppy Seed Cupcakes

You've heard of the muffins (maybe from a *Seinfeld* episode); now let me introduce the cupcakes. They are more moist and more flavorful than a typical muffin, yet gluten free and made with whole ingredients, including lots of my favorite citrus fruit: the lemon. I will admit that most of the name is simple marketing. What do you think people will be more excited to eat, a muffin or a cupcake? Nevertheless, whatever you call them, they are a scrumptious gluten-free dessert, snack, or breakfast.

makes 12 cupcakes

Grapeseed oil, for greasing

1 cup brown rice flour

1 cup white rice flour

2 teaspoons tapioca starch

1½ teaspoons baking powder

¼ teaspoon sea salt

⅔ cup almond meal

⅓ cup coconut oil, at room temperature

¾ cup organic cane sugar

2 large eggs

1 teaspoon vanilla extract

¼ cup fresh lemon juice

1 cup almond milk, homemade (page 34) or store-bought

2 tablespoons poppy seeds

Zest of 1 lemon

1¼ cups organic confectioners' sugar

1. Preheat the oven to 350°F. Grease a 12-cup muffin tin with grapeseed oil (or line with paper cupcake liners) and set aside.
2. Sift the rice flours, tapioca starch, baking powder, and salt into a medium bowl. Add the almond meal and stir to combine.
3. In the bowl of an electric mixer fitted with the whisk attachment, beat the coconut oil and sugar on high speed until well combined, 2 minutes. Add the eggs one at a time, beating after each addition. Beat in the vanilla and 2 tablespoons of the lemon juice. Add ½ cup of the dry ingredients and ¼ cup almond milk to the wet mixture and beat well. Repeat until all of the dry ingredients and the almond milk have been incorporated. Add the poppy seeds and lemon zest. Divide the batter among the prepared muffin cups.
4. Bake until a wooden skewer inserted into the center comes out clean, about 23 minutes. Let cool completely. Transfer the cupcakes from the tin to a piece of waxed paper.
5. Whisk together the confectioners' sugar and remaining 2 tablespoons lemon juice. Spoon the glaze over the cooled cupcakes and let set, about 5 minutes.

Stewed Apples

This is another modified version of Grandma's best that I am very proud of. I was able to make it as flavorful and rich as hers while keeping it vegan and gluten free. It's another of those recipes that I make for dessert, serving it with coconut ice cream or almond milk poured over the top, but then also eat for breakfast the next morning, without any guilt! If you look at the ingredients, you probably have them all in your cupboard right now. Be sure to make this with fresh-picked organic apples, if you can, and local maple syrup.

serves 6

5 medium organic apples, cored and sliced

1 cup fresh orange juice

¼ cup maple syrup

2 tablespoons coconut oil

½ teaspoon ground cinnamon

¼ teaspoon grated nutmeg

¼ teaspoon sea salt

½ cup crushed walnuts

1. In a large pot set over low heat, combine the apple slices, orange juice, maple syrup, coconut oil, cinnamon, nutmeg, and sea salt. Bring to a simmer, cover, and cook, stirring occasionally, for 30 minutes. Uncover the pot and cook, stirring occasionally, until the apples are soft, about 15 minutes.
2. Remove the pot from the heat, stir in the walnuts, and serve warm or chill for later.

november

Caramelized Pear Muffins

Huevos Rancheros

Eggplant and Chickpea Stew

Cream of Celery Soup

Wild Rice and Pecan Stuffing

Green Bean and Onion Casserole

Sweet Potato Pudding

Corn Bread with Spicy Honey Butter

Curried Cranberry Sauce

Real Pumpkin Pie, Vegan Style

Let's be honest: November is a total drag in Michigan. It's a good thing we have ***Thanksgiving*** in there, because otherwise we might all move away and never come back. I personally would like to spend November in Nicaragua, or Mexico, or anywhere south of Michigan, but because that's not possible, we make the most of it.

One remedy for November is to eat well—deliciously and healthfully. I have created ***recipes that make me feel like I'm indulging*** but in reality keep me eating healthy, whole foods that fill me up before I overeat. I love warm spices, squash of many kinds, and winter fruits like pears and cranberries. I will admit to getting a tad more over-the-top with my recipes—I figure I have a bit of leeway because I'll be in sweaters and coats for several more months.

Because we are indoors so much, I have lots of time to plan and test the ultimate Thanksgiving feast. I also have time to start getting my mandatory holiday chores done (like cards). Maybe there is a reason for the inability to play outside. Even though I get grumpy about it, it's probably good that we are forced to ***refocus and get things done inside***. After all, I always tell my friends in California one of the reasons we start companies here in Michigan is because we have so much time to think in the winter.

NOVEMBER

Here is a sample menu I've put together with
a variety of recipes for this month.

breakfast

Huevos Rancheros

•

lunch

Eggplant and Chickpea Stew

•

midday snack

Caramelized Pear Muffins

•

dinner

Wild Rice and Pecan Stuffing and
Green Bean and Onion Casserole

•

dessert

Real Pumpkin Pie, Vegan Style

Caramelized Pear Muffins

Caramelizing pears makes them incredibly decadent. The prep work on this one is so easy that it'll remind you how much better it is to make your own baked goods. When I look at the "homemade" muffins at the grocery store, they are filled with ingredients and chemicals I do not recognize. Keeping it simple is key, and proving to yourself that you can easily bake amazing foods builds confidence. These are super-simple, gluten free, and healthy for all. This recipe can also be a dessert served warm out of the oven and crumbled into bowls with coconut ice cream.

makes 12 muffins

3 ripe green pears, peeled, cored, and chopped

⅓ cup organic cane sugar

4 large egg whites

¼ cup grapeseed oil

¼ cup agave nectar

⅓ cup unsweetened applesauce

1 teaspoon almond extract

1½ cups almond meal

¾ cup coconut flour

2 teaspoons tapioca starch

1 teaspoon baking powder

¼ teaspoon sea salt

1. Preheat the oven to 325°F. Line a 12-cup muffin tin with paper liners.
2. In a medium skillet set over medium heat, combine the pears and sugar. Cook until lightly golden, about 10 minutes. Set aside to cool for 10 minutes.
3. In a medium bowl, whisk together the egg whites, oil, agave, applesauce, and almond extract.
4. In a large bowl, combine the almond meal, coconut flour, tapioca starch, baking powder, and salt. Make a well in the center of the dry ingredients, pour the egg white mixture into it, and stir until just combined. Fold in half of the pears. Spoon the batter into the prepared muffin cups. Top each with the remaining pears.
5. Bake until golden brown and puffed in the center, about 20 minutes. Let cool for 10 minutes before removing the muffins from the pan. Serve warm or at room temperature.

Huevos Rancheros

If I didn't know I was 100 percent Dutch, I would guess that there is Mexican heritage in me. I love the country, people, and food so much that I feel like I must have it in my blood. I have learned from visiting Mexico that the secret to their amazing food is the combination of fresh ingredients. When I go grocery shopping in Mexico, I am always impressed that everyone's shopping carts are filled with mostly fresh ingredients and very little processed food. Needless to say, their cooking and shopping manners have influenced me. Huevos rancheros is a breakfast favorite of mine. There is nothing like sleeping in late and creating a huge plate full of colorful, fresh veggies to start the day.

serves 4

1 (14.5-ounce) can black beans, rinsed and drained

½ cup chopped onion

3 plum tomatoes, chopped

1 medium ripe avocado, peeled, pitted, and sliced

2 tablespoons chopped fresh cilantro

Sea salt and freshly ground black pepper

8 corn tortillas

1 tablespoon grapeseed oil

4 large eggs

1. Combine the beans, onion, tomatoes, avocado, and cilantro in a medium bowl. Season with salt and pepper and set aside.
2. In a nonstick skillet set over medium heat, cook the tortillas, one at a time, until light golden in color, 30 seconds on each side. Transfer to a plate and cover loosely with a clean dish towel to keep warm.
3. Heat the grapeseed oil in the same nonstick skillet (or a well-seasoned cast-iron pan) set over medium-low heat. Crack the eggs into the skillet and cook until the whites are almost set with just a bit of raw whites on top. Cover and turn off the heat. Let stand to finish cooking, 2 to 3 minutes. Remove the pan from the heat.
4. To serve, put 2 tortillas on each plate. Top each plate with 1 egg and spoon the bean mixture evenly over the tops.

Eggplant *and* Chickpea Stew

This recipe has it all! Vegan protein, antioxidant-rich vegetables, herbs, and spices—you could practically live off this dish alone. Winter is such a wonderful time for stews with warm fragrant spices, and this one is a comfort food that you can be proud of. Garam masala is a spice that many people are not familiar with. It is most commonly used in Indian and Asian cuisines, and is a blend of sweet and hot spices like cinnamon, cumin, pepper, and cloves. It is similar to allspice except zestier. It makes this stew wonderfully fragrant.

serves 4 to 6

3 tablespoons grapeseed oil

1 medium red onion, cut into large chunks

4 Japanese eggplants, cut in half lengthwise and sliced into 1-inch pieces

1½ cups vegetable broth, homemade (see Tip, page 183) or store-bought

1 (16-ounce) can tomato sauce

1 (14.5-ounce) can chickpeas, rinsed and drained

4 large tomatoes, cored and coarsely chopped, juice reserved

2 large carrots, cut into 1-inch pieces

¼ cup brown lentils

1 teaspoon turmeric

1 teaspoon ground cumin

1 teaspoon garam masala

1 teaspoon sea salt

1 teaspoon freshly ground black pepper

½ cup chopped fresh cilantro leaves

2 tablespoons fresh lemon juice, or to taste

1. Heat the oil in a large pot or Dutch oven set over medium heat. Add the onion and eggplant and cook, stirring, for 15 minutes. Add the broth, tomato sauce, chickpeas, tomatoes and their juices, carrots, lentils, turmeric, cumin, garam masala, salt, and pepper. Bring to a boil over high heat. Reduce the heat to medium-low and simmer until the lentils are tender, about 25 minutes.

2. Remove the pan from the heat and stir in the cilantro and lemon juice. Let cool for 5 minutes before serving. Serve hot.

Cream of Celery Soup

Celery is one of the most inexpensive vegetables to buy. I have to admit, I am not a huge fan of plain celery, which is why you don't see it in many of my recipes. But I love all things creamy! This recipe is perfect because it is green like the celery and very rich from the avocado and almond milk. It's also dairy free and packed with antioxidant-rich vegetables. If you want to add a little color, garnish with a handful of chopped red and yellow peppers.

serves 2 to 4

2 tablespoons olive oil

3 cups chopped celery

1 cup chopped onion

2 tablespoons white whole-wheat flour

3 cups vegetable broth, homemade (see Tip, page 183) or store-bought

1 teaspoon sea salt, plus more to taste

1 cup unsweetened almond milk, homemade (page 34) or store-bought

2 teaspoons dry mustard

1 avocado, peeled, pitted, and chopped

1 teaspoon freshly ground black pepper, plus more to taste

Fresh parsley leaves, for garnish

1. Heat the oil in a large soup pot set over medium-low heat. Add the celery and onion and cook, stirring, until the onion is soft, about 15 minutes. Add the flour and stir until the flour is slightly brown, about 30 seconds. Slowly add the vegetable broth and cook until the soup is thick and the flour has dissolved, about 5 minutes. Add the salt and stir for 2 minutes. Remove the pan from the heat.
2. In a blender, working in batches if necessary, combine the soup, almond milk, dry mustard, avocado, and pepper. Blend until smooth.
3. Return the soup to the pan and warm it over low heat. Season to taste with salt and pepper and garnish with fresh parsley leaves. Serve warm.

tip *a vegetarian thanksgiving*

At first I thought that Thanksgiving was going to be a hard day for me as a vegetarian, worrying that I wouldn't be able to enjoy it without the turkey. But in reality, I did not even crave the turkey meat. The beautiful salads and colorful vegetables are more than enough to keep me happy. Once I started eating a more plant-based diet, my body led me further down that path by no longer craving animal-based foods.

I also realize that I am not alone! There are more than seven million vegetarians in the United States. Most of them cite animal welfare and overall health benefits as the major reason for choosing this lifestyle. That's great news for turkeys on Thanksgiving! Even more exciting for me is that many more Americans say they follow a "vegetarian-inclined" diet, meaning they dine on more plant-based foods and less meat. I also love that the younger generation is embracing vegetarianism. It all speaks well to our future health and compassion as a nation.

Wild Rice *and* Pecan Stuffing

When I was about six my uncle and aunt bought a microwave—they were the first in our family to own one. It was a huge, fascinating contraption and they were very proud of it. That year, they decided to have the entire family over for Thanksgiving, and guess what they were going to use to cook the turkey? That's right, their microwave. My aunt went on and on about how it would cook the massive bird in only a few hours. She didn't have to get up early!

We all waited with bated breath, and sure enough, after a few hours the turkey was done. As my aunt took it out, it was steamy and it smelled good, but it was still pink and looked kind of gross. Turns out it was as tough as could be! Needless to say, we never had a microwaved turkey again. Luckily, I don't have to deal with turkeys at all! This stuffing is hearty enough to be a main dish.

serves 4

$2\frac{1}{3}$ cups filtered water

1 cup wild rice

1 tablespoon grapeseed oil

2 large carrots, chopped

2 celery stalks, chopped

1 cup chopped red onion

$\frac{1}{2}$ teaspoon crushed fennel seeds

$\frac{1}{2}$ teaspoon sea salt

$\frac{1}{8}$ teaspoon cayenne pepper

2 cups chopped button mushrooms

2 garlic cloves, minced

$\frac{1}{3}$ cup coarsely chopped pecans

1. In a small saucepan set over high heat, bring the water and rice to a boil. Cover, reduce the heat to low, and cook until the water is absorbed and the rice is tender, about 50 minutes. Set aside, covered, for 10 minutes.

2. Heat the oil in a large skillet set over medium heat. Add the carrots, celery, onion, fennel seeds, salt, and cayenne and cook, stirring occasionally, until lightly golden, about 4 minutes. Add the mushrooms and garlic and cook, stirring, until the mushrooms are tender, about 4 minutes.

3. Remove the skillet from the heat and stir in the wild rice and pecans. Serve hot, at room temperature, or chilled.

Green Bean *and* Onion Casserole

Who doesn't love green bean casserole? This is truly one recipe that is so much better and delicious when made the healthy way! Using fresh green beans and sautéed fresh onions instead of packaged beans and fried onions from a can makes a world of difference. It's not a matter of missing anything—it's a matter of wondering why you ever made it the old way! It's a delicious, vegan, healthy twist on an old Thanksgiving classic.

serves 6 to 8

1 tablespoon grapeseed oil, plus more for frying

1 pound petite green beans, trimmed

1 tablespoon olive oil

1½ cups sliced small button mushrooms

1½ cups unsweetened almond milk, homemade (page 34) or store-bought

1 tablespoon tapioca starch

½ teaspoon sea salt

⅛ teaspoon freshly ground black pepper

2 medium onions, thinly sliced

1. Preheat the oven to 350°F. Grease a 9-inch square baking dish with 1 tablespoon of the grapeseed oil.
2. Bring a large saucepan of water to a boil over high heat. Add the green beans and cook until bright green, about 7 minutes. Drain and set aside.
3. Heat the olive oil in a medium skillet set over medium-high heat. Add the mushrooms and cook until golden, about 4 minutes. Whisk in the almond milk, tapioca starch, salt, and pepper and cook until thickened, about 7 minutes. Add the green beans and cook until the beans are completely tender, about 7 minutes. Let the mixture cool for 5 minutes, and then transfer to a serving dish. Bake for 15 to 20 minutes.
4. Meanwhile, spread the onion slices on several layers of paper towels and pat dry. Pour about ¼ inch of grapeseed oil into a small sauté pan and place it over medium-high heat. Working in batches, fry the onions until golden brown and crispy, about 2 minutes. Transfer to a paper towel–lined plate to drain. Sprinkle over the green bean mixture just before serving. Serve hot.

Sweet Potato Pudding

Grandma Vroon always brings her "Festive Sweet Potatoes" to Thanksgiving, and they are one of the first foods to be scarfed down. Rich and delicious, like a gourmet pudding, they are the hit of the meal. But the recipe is laden with sugar, butter, and eggs galore, and so, to keep it on my holiday table, I had to make some adjustments. Here is my remake of Grandma's yummy dish. No one even notices the difference!

serves 6 to 8

6 medium sweet potatoes

1 (14-ounce) package firm tofu

¾ cup honey

½ cup almond milk, homemade (page 34) or store-bought

3 tablespoons coconut oil

2 teaspoons vanilla extract

TOPPING

1 cup packed organic brown sugar

1 cup unsweetened coconut

1 cup chopped pecans

⅓ cup melted coconut oil

1. Preheat the oven to 400°F.
2. Pierce each potato several times with a fork and put them all on a rimmed baking sheet. Bake until a knife easily passes through them, 1 to 1¼ hours. Set aside until cool enough to handle.
3. Cut the potatoes in half and either pinch off the skins or scoop the flesh out with a spoon. Put the sweet potato flesh in the bowl of a food processor and add the tofu, honey, almond milk, coconut oil, and vanilla. Blend until smooth (you may have to do this in two batches). Spoon the mixture into a 9 × 13-inch baking dish.
4. For the topping, in a small bowl combine the brown sugar, coconut, pecans, and oil. Spread or sprinkle the topping over the sweet potato mixture.
5. Bake until the top is golden brown and the casserole is heated through, about 30 minutes.

Corn Bread *with* Spicy Honey Butter

Did you know that you can easily make your own corn bread with whole, organic, non-GMO ingredients? It only takes 15 minutes to assemble and comes in so handy when you want a side dish for your soup or salads but don't want plain bread. I make this to go with chili and to crumble over my Red Lentil Cumin Soup (page 186), Carrot and Curry Soup (page 58), and Cream of Celery Soup (page 197). The butter is optional, but, boy, does it take it over the top. The creamy, sweet, and spicy butter melted on the homemade corn bread is so good you could eat this as a dessert or even a breakfast! Often we eat it fresh out of the oven with no butter, only honey, and it's just as delicious.

serves 10

HONEY BUTTER

½ cup (1 stick) salted butter, at room temperature

1 tablespoon honey

⅛ teaspoon cayenne pepper

CORN BREAD

½ cup (1 stick) unsalted butter, melted, plus extra for greasing

1 large egg, slightly beaten

1 cup almond milk, homemade (page 34) or store-bought

¼ cup honey

2⅔ cups organic yellow cornmeal

¾ cup white whole-wheat flour

1 tablespoon baking powder

½ teaspoon baking soda

½ teaspoon sea salt

1. For the honey butter, in a medium bowl, combine the butter, honey, and cayenne. Cover and set aside or chill.
2. Preheat the oven to 375°F. Grease an 8 × 8-inch baking dish or cake pan with butter.
3. For the corn bread, whisk together the egg, almond milk, and honey. Whisk in the melted butter.
4. In a large bowl, combine the cornmeal, flour, baking powder, baking soda, and salt. Make a well in the center of the cornmeal mixture. Add the egg mixture and stir just until combined. Pour the batter into the prepared pan.
5. Bake until slightly puffed in the center and golden brown, about 25 minutes. Let cool on a wire rack before cutting.
6. Serve hot, warm, or at room temperature with the honey butter.

tip *genetically modified ingredients explained*

Non-GMO is a term that comes up more and more in the grocery stores and in the media, but it is confusing to many people. Because all of my company's products are certified non-GMO, I am very educated in what it means, and very passionate about why we should only eat non-GMO foods.

GMO stands for "genetically modified ingredients." Therefore, non-GMO means not genetically altered at all, or completely the way Mother Nature created it. Genetic modification is when scientists change a food's DNA, its genetic makeup, in a lab. This is different from crossbreeding species of similar plants, which is a natural way to create plants with genetic variation.

The foods that are most typically genetically modified in the United States are alfalfa, corn, soybeans, sugar beets, cotton, canola, papaya, and zucchini. If you look at the label of any processed food on the grocery store shelf, it most likely contains one of these ingredients or a derivative of one—especially soy, sugar, and corn.

So, what's the big deal? For me, it's the fact that many other countries, including Japan, Germany, France, Ireland, Switzerland, Australia, and New Zealand, restrict or ban the cultivation of GMO crops. They based their decisions on independent studies that have shown that GMO products can potentially affect fertility, lead to digestive problems, and interrupt normal development, as well as other possible unknown effects.

The best way to avoid GMOs is to buy organic foods and to look for the non-GMO verified seal. Organic farming does not allow the use of GMO seeds, and the non-GMO seal means the product has been tested and confirmed not to have such ingredients. Another way to avoid the altered stuff is to grow your own foods from organic heirloom seeds. Stay educated and do what you can to oppose the use of GMOs in our food supply so that it doesn't get worse than it already is.

Curried Cranberry Sauce

I love things with a twist, especially when your family and friends say, "This is so delicious . . . what's in here?" I get that all the time with dishes like this and my Watermelon Mint Salad (page 134), which have unexpected combinations. Mostly I come across these combinations by a process of trial and error. My poor family has been subjected to quite a few combos that don't actually work, but they've been good sports, and every once in a while I stumble across a mixture of herbs and spices that is just lovely. Here, I combine one of my beloved spices—curry—with a tangy-sweet cranberry orange sauce that is the perfect complement to any meal, or a great snack on its own.

makes about 3½ cups

1 (12-ounce) package fresh cranberries

1½ cups fresh orange juice

¾ cup maple syrup

¼ teaspoon allspice

½ teaspoon curry powder

1. In a saucepan set over medium-low heat, combine the cranberries, orange juice, and maple syrup. Bring to a gentle boil and cook, stirring occasionally, until the cranberries have popped and the juices have reduced, about 25 minutes. Remove the pan from the heat and let sit for 5 minutes.
2. To serve, pour the mixture into a serving dish and stir in the allspice and curry. Serve warm or chilled.

Real Pumpkin Pie, Vegan Style

It's very hard for me to use pumpkin out of a can for a pumpkin pie or any pumpkin recipe. The flavor of homemade roasted pumpkin is so far superior, and the fact that it is fresh from the farmer's market means it is better for you and the environment. This pumpkin pie is one of my favorite recipes. It is so easy and delicious and incredibly good for you. Pumpkin, unadulterated with fats and oils and combined with antioxidant-rich spices, creates a hearty and nutritious treat. The filling is so wonderful that I sometimes just make the filling, refrigerate it, and serve it as pumpkin pudding for dessert or as a fall side dish. The crust is as easy as throwing ingredients into your food processor and pushing a button. It is my all-time favorite go-to crust for any baked pie because it turns out perfect every time. Enjoy this dairy-free, antioxidant-powered, scrumptious fall gift!

makes one 9-inch pie

CRUST

1¼ cups white whole-wheat flour or organic all-purpose flour

2 teaspoons organic confectioners' sugar

¼ teaspoon sea salt

½ cup (1 stick) salted vegan buttery spread, chilled and cut into small pieces

3 tablespoons cold water

FILLING

2 cups homemade pumpkin purée (see Tip, page 185) or 1 (15-ounce) can pumpkin purée

1 (8-ounce) package firm tofu

1 teaspoon ground cinnamon

½ teaspoon ground ginger

¼ teaspoon ground cloves

½ teaspoon sea salt

¾ cup packed organic dark brown sugar

1. Preheat the oven to 350°F.
2. For the crust, in the bowl of a food processor, combine the flour, confectioners' sugar, and salt. Pulse 2 or 3 times to combine. Drop the pieces of butter into the flour mixture and pulse 3 or 4 times until partially combined. Drizzle in the water and pulse until the dough comes together into several pieces. Take the dough out of the food processor and form it into a 1-inch-thick disk. On a floured work surface, roll out the dough to fit a 9-inch pie dish. Press the dough evenly into the pie dish and set aside.
3. For the filling, in the clean bowl of a food processor, combine the pumpkin purée, tofu, spices, salt, and brown sugar. Process until smooth, about 20 seconds. Scoop the mixture into the pie crust.
4. Bake until the crust is golden brown and the filling is firm, about 1 hour. Let cool for 20 minutes before serving.

december

Roasted Hazelnut Granola

Asiago Jalapeño Muffins

Polenta with Currants and Allspice

Citrus and Pomegranate Salad

Parsnip and Thyme Cream Soup

Walnut-Stuffed Squash

Pumpkin Millet with Kale

Red Quinoa with Brussels Sprouts and Shallots

Peppermint Brownies

Vegan Eggnog

It's the last month of the year, but the first ***official month of winter***. We usually see our first snow of the season, and no matter how much we complain, this month is magical. I think we never quite lose the excitement we had for December as children. It means time away from school, playing in the first snow, twinkling Christmas lights against the white landscape, great movies, cozy houses, and wonderful seasonal ***food shared with loved ones***.

I remember the excitement of going to Grandma and Grandpa Otten's house for our extended family Christmas. There were seven of us little grand-girls, and every year Grandma and Grandpa bought seven of something wonderful. One year we all got "Baby Alive Dolls," and the next year we got handmade rocking cradles for the dolls (which I still have). The next year we received matching pink velvet bathrobes. It was always such a joy! Grandma and Grandpa lived in a tiny house with only six rooms, and when we all gathered there, it was a ***house filled with love and laughter***.

December is a great month to have your oven on. Roasting, baking, and cooking of all sorts make your house smell wonderful, and that's what this month is all about. Juicy citrus, rich walnuts, warm hearty stews, sweet peppermint, dark chocolate, and spicy eggnog help define this ***enchanting season***.

DECEMBER

Here is a sample menu I've put together with a variety of recipes for this month.

breakfast

Polenta with Currants and Allspice

•

lunch

Parsnip and Thyme Cream Soup

•

midday snack

Asiago Jalapeño Muffins

•

dinner

Red Quinoa with Brussels Sprouts and Shallots

•

dessert

Peppermint Brownies

Roasted Hazelnut Granola

Making your own granola can be intimidating because it seems like something only the most devoted naturalists would do. However, just like many other recipes, it is actually easy and the rewards are immense. Most granola is very expensive and not very good for you. Like many other food products made commercially, unnecessary ingredients, many of them unnatural, are added. There are always exceptions, though you'll probably pay a high cost for it.

My granola can be made in well under an hour and will keep for three weeks in your cupboard. It is much healthier and much less expensive than store-bought. I usually make a big recipe with the kids as a Christmas break activity.

serves 4 to 5

2 tablespoons grapeseed oil, plus more for greasing

⅔ cup coarsely chopped hazelnuts

1½ cups rolled oats

¼ cup coconut flour

¼ cup almond meal

⅛ teaspoon grated nutmeg

½ cup agave nectar

⅓ cup dried cherries

1. Preheat the oven to 350°F.
2. Grease a baking sheet with oil. Spread the hazelnuts on the baking sheet and bake until toasted and a golden color, about 6 minutes. Transfer to a medium bowl and set aside.
3. Reduce the oven temperature to 300°F.
4. In a medium bowl, combine the oats, coconut flour, almond meal, and nutmeg. Stir in the agave and 2 tablespoons oil. Spread the mixture evenly on the same baking sheet.
5. Bake until golden and dry, about 30 minutes. Stir in the cherries and hazelnuts and let cool completely. Store in an airtight container for up to 3 weeks.

Asiago Jalapeño Muffins

Raise your hand if you like cold pizza for breakfast! I am definitely a fan of a savory breakfast. You will catch me eating hummus and pita and last night's leftovers for breakfast all the time. If you can relate, you will enjoy these muffins for breakfast as well. I particularly love unique and surprising flavors, and these muffins definitely deliver on a punch of the wonderfully unexpected. I developed these especially for my ten-year-old son, Noah, who would eat an Asiago cheese bagel for breakfast every morning if he could. I spread soft goat cheese on them warm out of the oven and it beats a bagel every time!

makes 12 mini muffins

Grapeseed oil or coconut oil spray, for greasing

½ cup brown rice flour

½ cup almond meal

½ teaspoon baking soda

⅛ teaspoon sea salt

½ ripe avocado, peeled and pitted

⅓ cup almond milk, homemade (page 34) or store-bought

1 large egg

¼ cup grated Asiago cheese

3 teaspoons minced jalapeño pepper

6 thin slices jalapeño pepper, cut in half, for garnish

1. Preheat the oven to 325°F. Grease a mini muffin pan with oil and set aside.
2. In a medium bowl, whisk together the rice flour, almond meal, baking soda, and salt. Set aside.
3. In the bowl of a food processor, combine the avocado, almond milk, and egg and process until very smooth, about 45 seconds. Slowly add the rice flour mixture to the food processor, pulsing between additions, until the mixture is smooth. Scrape down the sides of the bowl with a rubber spatula, if necessary. Add 3 tablespoons of the Asiago cheese and the minced jalapeño, and pulse once or twice to combine. The batter should be the consistency of bread dough. Spoon the batter into the prepared mini muffin tins. Sprinkle the tops with the remaining 1 tablespoon Asiago cheese and 1 slice of jalapeño.
4. Bake until lightly golden and puffed in the center, 15 to 17 minutes. Serve warm or at room temperature.

Polenta *with* Currants *and* Allspice

Organic polenta is a great addition to your breakfast repertoire. It is hearty comfort food, providing protein, fiber, and lots of iron, yet easy to prepare and very versatile. It is delicious as a sweet or savory dish. I love eating it alongside eggs, sprinkled with Parmesan and drizzled with olive oil, while my kids like it sweetened with fruit and maple syrup or agave, as in this delicious recipe.

serves 4

3 cups almond milk, homemade (page 34) or store-bought

1 cup polenta

¼ cup currants, plus more for garnish

2 tablespoons coconut oil

⅛ teaspoon sea salt

2 tablespoons agave nectar, plus more for garnish

⅛ teaspoon ground cinnamon

Pinch of ground allspice

1. In a medium saucepan set over high heat, bring 2 cups of the almond milk to a boil. Add the polenta, currants, coconut oil, and salt, stirring quickly to combine. Reduce the heat to medium-low and simmer, stirring occasionally, until all the liquid has been absorbed, about 5 minutes.

2. Remove the pan from the heat and stir in the agave, cinnamon, and allspice. Pour ¼ cup of the remaining 1 cup almond milk in the bottom of each of 4 serving bowls and spoon the hot polenta over the top. Garnish with the currants and drizzle with agave. Serve immediately.

Citrus *and* Pomegranate Salad

When I first start to see pomegranates at the store, I buy three or four each week. I try to eat or incorporate one of this truly seasonal fruit into our diet often for as long as they are around. Pomegranates are extremely high in antioxidants, which have been shown to improve cardiovascular function, help prevent disease, and improve mental health. This salad marries two extremely nutritious foods together in a brightly colored and incredibly healthy dish. With all of the heavy holiday food that surrounds us in December, I crave this light and juicy salad, and I love bringing it to holiday parties as a stunning and healthy yet festive dish.

serves 8

2 large grapefruit, peeled
3 large oranges, peeled
Seeds of 1 pomegranate
¼ cup sweetened coconut flakes

Slice the grapefruit and oranges into thin rounds. Layer the fruit slices in a glass serving bowl and sprinkle the pomegranate seeds over the top. Scatter the coconut flakes on top and serve.

tip citrus

In the winter months, citrus is plentiful! I love how Mother Nature makes sure we have fresh produce all year round that meets our needs. In the months when colds and flu take hold, we have fruits high in vitamin C and antimicrobial properties to help us ward off infection. These fruits also contain compounds called citrus limonoids, which have been shown in laboratory studies to help protect us against certain types of cancer and help lower cholesterol.

Citrus is inexpensive and wonderful to cook with. I try to eat an orange or a grapefruit every day, or squeeze some lemon into my meals, to take advantage of their many health benefits. I also like that citrus fruits have a longer shelf life than many fruits and can stay fresh in your refrigerator for several weeks.

Parsnip *and* Thyme Cream Soup

Sometimes I wonder how the carrot became so popular while its close relative, the parsnip, is practically unknown. Parsnips may be much less colorful than carrots, but they are actually sweeter, especially when cooked. You can substitute parsnips in most of your carrot recipes if you're looking to switch things up a bit. They are delicious when roasted with honey and mustard or boiled until soft and topped with a little salt and butter. This soup is a favorite at my home. I love sending the kids out to the early spring garden to pick thyme leaves that stay green all winter.

serves 6

4 to 6 small parsnips, cut into ½-inch-thick rounds (2 cups)

3 tablespoons grapeseed oil

1 teaspoon sea salt

1 large onion, chopped

3 cups unsalted vegetable broth, homemade (see Tip, page 183) or store-bought

2 cups almond milk, homemade (page 34) or store-bought

2 tablespoons fresh thyme leaves

Freshly ground black pepper

1. Preheat the oven to 400°F.
2. In a large bowl, toss the parsnips with 1 tablespoon of the grapeseed oil and the salt. Transfer to a baking dish. Roast until soft, 20 to 30 minutes.
3. Meanwhile, heat 2 tablespoons of the oil in a soup pot set over medium-low heat. Add the onion and cook, stirring, until the onion is soft, about 10 minutes. Stir in the vegetable broth and almond milk. Add the roasted parsnips and bring to a gentle boil.
4. Working in batches, purée the soup in a blender or Vitamix until smooth. Return the soup to the pot and stir in the thyme. Season with pepper and serve warm.

Walnut-Stuffed Squash

Walnuts are one of my favorite foods because they are rich and satisfying but not overwhelming in flavor, so they blend well with many dishes. I also try to use walnuts whenever possible because they're packed with omega-3 fatty acids, which my family needs to get through plant sources because we don't eat fish.

Omega-3 fatty acids are extremely important for proper brain development. Studies have shown that children with good omega-3 intake do better in school and have fewer behavioral problems. Omega-3s are also instrumental in promoting cardiovascular health, reducing inflammation, and help to protect against certain kinds of cancer. They are an imperative part of our diet.

serves 4

2 tablespoons grapeseed oil, plus more for greasing

4 whole acorn or butternut squashes

1 cup thinly sliced onion

1 cup peeled and finely chopped parsnip

2 firm sweet apples (such as Gala, Fuji, or Pink Lady)

1 teaspoon curry powder

1 teaspoon sea salt

¼ teaspoon freshly ground black pepper

1 cup chopped shiitake mushrooms

2 tablespoons chopped fresh flat-leaf parsley

1 cup chopped walnuts

1. Preheat the oven to 375°F. Grease a small baking sheet generously with grapeseed oil.
2. Cut 1 inch off the tops of the acorn squashes, and reserve the tops. Scoop out the seeds and all but ½ inch of the flesh from the inside. Discard the seeds and finely chop the flesh; set aside. Put the squash shells cut-side down on the baking sheet and bake until tender, 35 to 37 minutes. Let cool.
3. Heat the oil in a large skillet set over medium-high heat. Add the onion, parsnip, apples, curry powder, salt, and pepper. Cook, stirring, until the onions are soft, about 4 minutes. Add the mushrooms and reserved squash flesh and cook until lightly golden, about 4 minutes. Remove the pan from the heat and stir in the parsley and walnuts. Set aside.
4. Turn the squash shells right side up on the baking sheet and spoon the filling into each. Place the reserved tops on the baking sheet beside the filled shells.
5. Bake until tender and the stuffed squashes begin to brown, about 15 minutes. Serve hot, with the squash "lid" next to the squash on the plate.

Pumpkin Millet *with* Kale

Millet is one of my go-to grains because it is easy, different, and delicious. It provides a nice variety from rice and quinoa. As a whole grain it is extremely healthy and packed with antioxidants, fiber, and magnesium. It cooks up similar to rice but with a subtle, nutty flavor.

What I love most about cooking with millet is that it really soaks up the spices and flavors around it. This particular dish may be the healthiest dish in this cookbook because of the whole-grain millet, the pumpkin, the kale, and all of the incredibly nutritious spices.

serves 4 to 5

3 cups filtered water

1 teaspoon sea salt

1 cup millet, rinsed

1 (2½-pound) pumpkin or 1 (2-pound) butternut squash, peeled and cut into ½-inch pieces

2 tablespoons grapeseed oil

1 teaspoon ground cumin

1 teaspoon ground coriander

1 bunch kale, tough stems removed and coarsely chopped

¼ teaspoon freshly ground black pepper

1. In a small saucepan set over high heat, bring the water, ½ teaspoon salt, and the millet to a boil. Reduce the heat to medium-low and cook until all of the water has been absorbed, 25 to 30 minutes. Remove the pan from the heat and set aside.

2. Meanwhile, bring a large saucepan of water to a boil over high heat. Add the pumpkin, reduce the heat to medium-low, cover, and cook until tender, about 12 minutes. Drain and set aside.

3. Heat the oil in a large skillet set over medium-high heat. Add ½ teaspoon of the cumin and ½ teaspoon of the coriander. Add the kale and the remaining ½ teaspoon salt and cook, stirring, until wilted, 4 to 5 minutes.

4. Transfer the cooked millet to a large bowl and add the remaining ½ teaspoon of cumin and coriander, and the pepper. Add the cooked pumpkin and kale, and toss well. Season with salt and pepper to taste and serve hot or at room temperature.

Red Quinoa *with* Brussels Sprouts *and* Shallots

Red quinoa is a beautiful grain to cook with, and as a complete vegan protein, it provides stellar nutrients. I love the colors in this dish and make it with farmer's market Brussels sprouts and thyme from my garden when possible. The champagne or white wine vinegar adds a tangy twist to the soft and sweet Brussels sprouts.

serves 4 to 6

2 cups filtered water

½ teaspoon sea salt, plus more to taste

1 cup red quinoa, rinsed and drained

2 tablespoons grapeseed oil

1 cup thinly sliced shallots

1 pound Brussels sprouts, trimmed and quartered

1 tablespoon chopped fresh thyme

1 tablespoon champagne or white wine vinegar

1 teaspoon crushed red pepper flakes

1. In a medium saucepan set over high heat, combine the water, salt, and quinoa. Bring to a boil, cover, reduce the heat to low, and cook until all the water has been absorbed, 15 to 20 minutes. Set aside.
2. Heat 1 tablespoon of the oil in a large skillet set over medium-high heat. Add the shallots and cook, stirring frequently, until soft, about 2 minutes. Add the remaining 1 tablespoon oil, Brussels sprouts, and thyme and cook, stirring occasionally, until tender, 8 to 10 minutes. Remove the pan from the heat.
3. Add the cooked quinoa to the skillet and stir well. Add the vinegar and red pepper flakes, and season with salt. Serve hot.

Peppermint Brownies

Sometimes a girl just needs a brownie. But if I could have one that's as easy to prepare as boxed mixes but without all of the extra processed ingredients, I'd be set. And they could also be gluten and dairy free and still melt in my mouth—that would be even better!

My dreams have come true with this recipe. Organic rice flour and coconut oil beautifully replace highly processed ingredients with ease. These brownies make living a healthy, balanced life so sweet and easy! People never guess that they contain no gluten or dairy. And the touch of peppermint extract makes them wonderfully festive for the holiday season.

makes one 8-inch square pan

Grapeseed oil or coconut oil spray, for greasing

½ cup white rice flour

½ cup brown rice flour

2 teaspoons tapioca starch

1 teaspoon baking powder

¼ teaspoon sea salt

½ cup coconut oil, at room temperature

1½ cups organic cane sugar, blended (see page 9)

¾ cup unsweetened cocoa powder

½ teaspoon vanilla extract

½ teaspoon peppermint extract

4 large eggs

1 cup chopped walnuts

1. Preheat the oven to 325°F. Grease an 8-inch square baking dish with oil and line the bottom with a piece of parchment paper. Set aside.
2. In a medium bowl, whisk together the white and brown rice flours, tapioca starch, baking powder, and salt.
3. In the bowl of an electric mixer fitted with the whisk attachment or using a handheld mixer, beat the coconut oil and sugar on medium speed until well combined, about 2 minutes. Add the cocoa powder, vanilla, and peppermint extract and beat until incorporated. Add the eggs one at a time, beating well after each addition. Add the flour mixture ½ cup at a time, beating until just combined. Stir in the walnuts and spread the batter in the prepared pan.
4. Bake until a toothpick inserted into the center comes out nearly clean, about 40 minutes. Let cool to room temperature before cutting and serving.

tip green holiday decorating

"Mom! I'm bored!" How many times will you hear this over the holiday break? Luckily, there are lots of DIY decorating crafts that you can do with your family to spend time, instead of money. Here are my favorites!

BRANCH CHRISTMAS TREE: Cut interesting branches from a tree or bush that are sturdy enough to hold ornaments. Arrange them in a large vase or pot or hang on the wall and decorate with ornaments.

SNOWFLAKES: Teach your kids how to make paper snowflakes and decorate your house with these little gems.

POPCORN AND CRANBERRY GARLAND: Revive old-fashioned decorating with this classic craft. If you're worried about kids handling needles, put a thimble on their fingers and let them string up popped popcorn and raw cranberries.

DRIFTWOOD OR SCRAP WOOD CHRISTMAS TREE: With some nails and a hammer you can create your own rustic Christmas tree to hang ornaments on. Simply nail pieces of wood together in the shape of a pine tree and decorate.

MAKE YOUR OWN CANDLES: Buy beeswax (you can find it at craft stores) and melt several chunks in a double boiler. Pour it into small glass Ball jars, old jam jars, honey jars, single muffin tins, or any cute creative container that won't melt. Keep a wick (also found at craft stores) centered in place by hanging it from a bobby pin laid across the mouth of the jar. Let cool until solid. Beeswax smells like honey as it melts when the candle is burning.

Vegan Eggnog

Although I'm not a big fan of eggs, around the holidays, I don't want to be left out of any eggnog drinking. So I set out to create an eggless version that would hit all the right flavor and texture notes, while also managing to be healthier and dairy free. This recipe is a lot easier to make than the traditional stuff because the process is so streamlined. Just throw it all in the blender and voilà! Oh, and just for the record, each serving contains only 150 calories and 2.5 grams of fat (compared with regular eggnog, which has 343 calories and 19 grams of mostly saturated fat). You can actually indulge in this eggless nog!

serves 4

2 cups almond milk, homemade (page 34) or store-bought

¼ cup spiced rum (optional)

½ teaspoon ground cinnamon

½ teaspoon grated nutmeg

¼ teaspoon vanilla extract

⅛ teaspoon sea salt

½ to 1 cup ice

In a blender, combine the almond milk, rum, cinnamon, nutmeg, vanilla, salt, and ice. Blend on low speed until smooth and serve immediately.

Acknowledgments

I am well aware that what I have accomplished in life is due to the beautiful and brilliant individuals who have walked alongside me through various parts of this journey. Their support, love, knowledge, experience, belief in me, and inspiration has led me and continues to propel me forward.

Thanks to my grandparents for living joyful, simple lives and for teaching me so many lessons in the kitchen and beyond. I am eternally grateful to my mom and dad, Anton and Jane Vroon, for their unconditional love and support and for modeling a life rich in love, not possessions.

I am humbled and blessed by my three beautiful children—Anna, Aleah, and Noah—who taught me the meaning of love and are the inspiration for everything good I do. Thank you for your honest assessments of my recipes, for being good sports through this process, and, more important, for keeping me ever focused on the big picture of love, life, and family.

To my remarkable husband, Kevin, who is my foundation, the one who upholds me, my forever partner, I am in awe of what we share. Thank you for loving me and my cooking so much!

I am thankful for my dear friends Myka, Diane, and Kristin for providing constant emotional support and always being willing to open a bottle of wine and pick up where we left off.

My heartfelt gratitude goes to these amazing partners in the Pure Food project:

Simon Goode and the Promax team, for your confidence in this book and my abilities, and for continuously helping the process move forward.

Amy Stanton, Leah Vail Soloff, and the Stanton ladies, for planting the seed of possibility for this book and holding my hand along the way, and beyond!

Dianne Jacob, for expertly walking me through the very beginnings of writing a book.

Coleen O'Shea, my literary agent extraordinaire, for believing in the opportunity at hand, always making yourself available to me, and having the business savvy to bring my voice and this project to the next level.

The late Liz Scott, whose final gift in life was helping me shape my proposal beautifully through her vast experience and knowledge of the industry. It is a treasure and gift beyond comprehension that I will always cherish.

Denise Vivaldo, Cindie Flannigan, and your awesome team for the creativity, hard work, sense of food style, and understanding of my vision for the book.

My editor, Ashley Phillips, for appreciating and encouraging my writing style, helping me to understand each phase, and having an eye for detail that shaped our book so perfectly. You are so talented!

The entire Clarkson Potter team for your skilled work and outstanding professional knowledge that helped to craft a cookbook we can all be very proud of.

Quentin Bacon and his crew for exquisite photography that blew my mind and brought life and beauty to these recipes.

Finally, I am forever grateful for our customers, my community, and all the lovely and amazing people who support the Pure brand and believe in a healthy Earth, a healthy body, and making a difference. Thank you for taking this journey with me and inspiring me every day.

Index